The Ontological I
&
Other Essays

Donovan Irven

Streisguth | Martin
Philadelphia, Pennsylvania
First Edition, May 2012

Cover Art and Design by
Steven Streisguth
Streisguth.com

Copyright © 2012 Donovan Irven
All rights reserved.
ISBN: 0984815902
ISBN-13: 978-0984815906

For my parents; all of them.

CONTENTS

	Acknowledgments	i
	Introduction	v
1	PRELUDE	1
2	THE ONTOLOGICAL I	
	First Study: Introduction to the Problem	5
	Second Study: Aporetic Origins	23
	Third Study: Circumspect Origins	48
	Fourth Study: Negative Ontology	70
	Fifth Study: Openness and Alterity	95
	Concluding Study	119
3	INTERLUDE	137
4	ON THE FREEDOM OF ACTION	
	Prolegomena	145
	The Possibility of Responsible Freedom	164
5	ETHICS IN REBELLION	195
6	NIHILISM AND ARCHETYPE	213
7	THE FREE SPIRIT PARALLAX	219
	Bibliography	237

ACKNOWLEDGMENTS

Much thanks and appreciation goes to Dr. Helen Schroepfer whose advice and critical support was integral in the development of the insights put forth in this work; many of which were exceedingly difficult to put into words. Dr. Matthew Pierlott must be acknowledged for keeping this work on track with current scholarship and for patiently seeing me through unnecessary verbiage to obtain a heightened sense of rigor and philosophical intelligence. I cannot thank Dr. Ruth Porritt enough for encouraging the creative and literary aspects of this thesis and for her help in not only finding, but in maintaining my own voice throughout the long writing process.

Among my fellows, I want to acknowledge Gabrielle Aruta, Corinne Lecourieux, Hilary Nunes, Anton Shannon, S Justus Bernard, Casey Giovinco, and Timothy Burke for their diligent support and criticism and for endless hours of conversation dedicated to the topics explored in these essays. For their friendship I will be always in their debt.

THE ONTOLOGICAL I
&
OTHER ESSAYS

INTRODUCTION

We have no philosophies but merely commentaries...considering that the age of philosophers concerned with philosophy was followed by the age of professors of philosophy concerned with philosophers. Such an attitude shows both modesty and impotence. And a thinker who began his books with these words: "Let us take things from the beginning," would evoke smiles. It has come to the point where a book of philosophy appearing today without basing itself on any authority, quotation, or commentary would not be taken seriously. And yet...[1]

He who wants to learn to philosophize must...regard all systems of philosophy only as the history of the use of reason and objects for exercising philosophical talent. The true philosopher, as self-thinker, thus must make free, not slavishly imitating use of his reason.[2]

The central theme of this book is the two thousand year refrain of the chorus of philosophy: Know Thyself! The perennial question is an existential one—who am I, what am I doing, what is the purpose of my life, am I responsible, am I free? All of these questions stem from that habit of the I to turn in on itself, to take the same analytic tools applied to the world and apply them to the Self. To know the Self! To care for the Self, to develop character, to be just—to learn to be free.

Further, no philosopher can move forward without first settling a few of these very questions for herself. Without first establishing a theory of the human person any philosophy is moving forward on baseless assumption, blindly making onto-epistemological assumptions which inform the implied metaphysics behind the theory. Central to any thesis of political, economic, social, ethical, environmental, religious, feminist, phenomenological, analytic, or deconstructive philosophy is an implicit theory of the human person and his or her capabilities as a thinking thing. What and how am I capable of perceptions, what are intentions and how do they relate to my actions, are my actions free or not, am I free to act in accordance with my own Will, etc. The answers to these questions are more frequently assumed by philosophical theory than they form philosophical theories themselves; at least those being put forward in this first decade of the twenty-first century.

Economics appears of central importance, and rightfully so given the events unfolding throughout the Reagan, Bush, and Clinton Presidencies, coming to a head in the fall of 2008. But again, economics concerns the study of an economy in operation among people and the human person inhabits the central position of any economic theory as the consumer, capitalist, laborer, and regulator all in one being—and one type of being capable of fulfilling this manifold of functionalities. Feminist and multicultural perspectives became a focus of academic development and curriculum restructuring in the latter half of the twentieth century, and in the early twenty-first century they are easily recognized as core values of a liberal arts education. Again, feminism and multiculturalism rooted in the diversified expression of the human person, that singular being capable of existing as man or woman, black or white, the speaker of one language or many, old and young, rich and poor, the Subject of all our predicates. The humanities are nothing without the human and rather than abandon the human person to psychology and reduce us to the functions of the brain detailed in neurological and cognitive sciences, I aim with this work insistent on a return of the human person to philosophy—a discipline frequently sterilized, in assumed objectivity, of the presence of the I.

But objectivity, if it is to be obtained, will not be grasped through the erasure of the I. In fact, the non-objectivity of the theory is exposed most frequently by the conspicuous absence of the I. The disembodied voice that misunderstood the meaning of "disinterested" distracts us from the theory, from the content and the form, to the strange vacuity of the speaker, of the author veiled behind a scaffolding of language and blinded in review.

This conspicuous absence is rendered as a sacrifice of the work of philosophy to a procedure of institution. Philosophy then becomes divorced from thinking, thus becoming non-philosophy, and reverts to whatever is the outcome of certain procedures occurring within an institution. The paper is written, not for philosophy, but only for the journal. The criteria imposed upon the philosophic work is external to the work and judges not whether the work fits into the canon of reason, but whether or not the work fits into the canon of the history of philosophy (but only the version of the canon reduced to the interests of the journal). Logic is not democratic: she is a cruel tyrant whether or not one's footnotes are in order and the most rigorously supported argument is not improved a fraction by the addition of Plato, just as Kant, Hegel, nor all the rest can save a false argument from the judgment of Truth by the inscription of a superscript numeral.

The war for objectivity—and to those post-moderns too squeamish of violence to admit war, I assure you one must wage a righteous struggle for the austerity of the objective—the war for objectivity can only be won through the clear and definitive acknowledgment of the self that spins the web of reason about a world experienced through the lens of conscious perception. Only by sacrificing the self at the center of this web can objectivity be presumed, and then only a presumption. By reducing the self, we merely banish him to a cave beneath the earth and thereby declare "out of sight, out of mind—on with business…" But it is the subject, the self, that carries on with business, only now he must carry on in ignorance of his own effects. The reduction of the Self misinterprets the sacrifice required by objectivity. It is the sacrifice to disinterestedness, i.e. that I must be careful to avoid my prejudices, especially that prejudice which persuades me that I am free of all prejudice! Those prejudices regarding myself are the most dangerous of all and to know thyself is to banish these prejudices under the light of reason turned on myself, ringing myself with the shock of the Question: "Who are you and what are you doing?"

Who am I? That has everything to do with the writing and reading of the current work. You will find, occasionally, autobiographical reflections alongside philosophic argumentation. Part of this results from the phenomenological methods employed, but a larger part still is the confessional nature of truly philosophizing. I speak, and my theory follows my speech, it is, really, my theory, even when I borrow from Aristotle. A philosopher is never more truthful because she did not speak. The voice of a philosopher gives form to truth and to falsehood and the tongue as well as the mind is the wielder of the sword and shield of logic—defender and slayer of the dragon, Theses. Sometimes, I am a commentator, and I commentate on what I've actually read, and these readings are part of my life narrative. At such and such a time, I studied such and such and read this book. And so the philosophical comes about through the recognition that my commentary is really a commentary on my reading and not on the work itself which appears to me only as an object in the world, it happens that the object is composed of symbols arranged in a certain fashion by some author, an author very often disconnected from me by death and time. But my commentary is not commentary on Kant; it is an analysis of my reading of the work produced by Kant so long ago. Thus, my writing is not an exegesis, strictly speaking, of the history of philosophy but an exegesis on how the history of philosophy has led me finally to the free use of my own reason, a reason common to humanity, or at the very least, since I am obliged to be post-post-modern, it is a reason available to the use of all people.

In order to be free in my use of this reason, which will not permit my willful misuse of it since the purposeful application of it destroys contradictions as a matter of function, I have foregone the usual institutional procedures regarding the publication of academic work. Since democracy is touted as the operating paradigm of social virtue in our times, lets us live our ideals and submit the work as it is to a democratic process, where whatever reason common to all people may judge the value of the work herein. In this domain, freed from the distractions of editorial commitments, may the tribunal of reason lay praise or blame at my feet for having produced a work for which only I am held accountable.

After all, the essay central to this volume, "The Ontological I," passed a rigorous peer review process already. That longer essay originally served as my Master's Thesis at West Chester University of Pennsylvania. Since that time, the work has again undergone many revisions, expanding on the sections of work original to my own thought and revising sections where references to the work of other philosophers could be clarified or better explained.

Versions of the essay "The Subject in Rebellion" were presented at philosophical conferences twice, and the Study from "The Ontological I" entitled "Circumspect Origins" was the subject of a guest lecture, delivered by myself, at Rutgers University of New Jersey. The essay "The Freedom of Action" was presented, in nascent form, at philosophy conferences and as a guest lecture, and a more complete version of that paper served as a research project in a seminar on the metaphysics of freedom. All of the works presents here appeared, in some early form, as the product of academic discourse on the themes of identity, freedom, and ethics. In a certain sense, this work has been thoroughly peer reviewed.

In another sense, however, and in a more important one, this work openly ignores what is commonly meant by "peer review." The reason for this is twofold. The first concerns the thematics of the work itself, and the second concerns the freedom of the author to write philosophy beyond the confines of institutional approval. When considering the existential questions surrounding my own being, that fact that there exists a canon of writings qualified as "philosophical" which deal at length with questions concerning human existence is of very little relevance. Each person is faced anew with existential concerns and is again equipped with whatever abilities the human mind may possess to cope with such issues. However, when dealing with existential quandaries, one thing people often do is read books that have been written about the subject. Such books might be explicitly philosophical, essays or treatises and the like, or they may be of a more literary quality, novels, plays, poems, etc. Therefore, I care very much what certain books that I have actually read say about the Self. Yet, no work that I've read presents as particularly true due to the citation it contains. Spinoza had very good points all on his own, without regard to Hegel who would come after, and Emmanuel Levinas does a fine job thinking all without referring to Derek Parfit, though my reading of the two together gave me much food for my own thought. And though the content of my thought be idiosyncratic, the form and structure of that content must oblige the laws of logic to test it. Logic itself gives rise to no new knowledge, but is only the tool by which one must judge the deductions we make beginning from ourselves, from principles originally derived from having actually done something. I read these books, and thought these things, and I am writing them down. I take responsibility for my work; it's not for some board to decide that they'll take responsibility as well. My words and writing are my deeds and no one need approve them with the rubber stamp of "philosophical." The stamp of the philosophical is in the use of reason and the insignia of those institutions that fancy themselves the vanguard of Reason are only the insignia of allegiances that are social allegiances, all surpassed by the philosopher's allegiance to truth and blind sacrifice of his own interest to the truth beyond the vanguard. The philosopher must be free, even in spite of the vanguard, for the freedom of thought never permitted an easy road for philosophy or her lover.

Thematically, the work is not in favor today. The style of the book may be overly literary. William Faulkner, Vladimir Nobakov, Walt Whitman, Richard Wright, these are not the names of "philosophers." Nonsense. Whoever thinks to judge these writers "not philosophers" is the enemy of philosophy and of free thought, and an enemy of the self whose own cowardice prevents the introspection demanded by the refrain "Know Thyself!" The chorus of philosophy is a thousand voices deep; its cavernous refrain is difficult to ignore. Derrida, Parfit, Searle, Ricoeur, Irigaray, Chisholm, Dennett, Levinas, Korsgaard—these names do not go together! The analytics pass over in silence and the continentals say nothing at all! Whosoever agrees with judgments such as these is a fool, and an enemy of philosophy, and worse: the corruptor of the youth who long for philosophers but find only the quibbling of lesser men. The chorus of philosophy is a thousand voices deep; one must merely train oneself to recognize the tenor of truth in each voice. None are quite so easily disregarded. I point out here the prejudices of professors of philosophy who are not themselves quite capable of philosophizing. Best to ignore or pass over or obfuscate than to learn to listen and reason—what rubbish. And yet any true philosopher would be asked to submit his work for the approval of sycophants. How could the philosopher not convulse with disdain at the thought?

To take the road to true philosophy the philosopher must be willing to forego the comforts of approval and the glow that comes from acceptance—oh, the longed for acceptance letter!—and be prepared to speak for themselves and be the free thinker that is the rightful midwife to any true thought. One does not deliver in chains.

I know that in regard to some of the preceding points there will be those so-called philosophers who will say, "Poor Donovan Irven, he must have been rejected from very many journals to think this way!" But they will not know that I have submitted none of the essays contained in this book for publication in an academic journal. None of these essays have been rejected in their current form.

But more to the point, those who would level psychological criticism at me betray their own bias by employing the ad hominem fallacy. Only a failure to listen, to read, to approach the work as it reads and to meet theory with theory would result in such gross dismissal of an independent philosopher. Sycophants, bad philosophers, and sophists—all those afraid that philosophy might be born in the world beyond the university, as if they could admit such a world exists! Do not mistake my polemics as being the ravings of a disenfranchised academic. I love the academy and have met with much success as well as failure in my academic pursuits. Few are those scholars, even among the canonized, who are successful in their craft without facing and overcoming challenges. I would not destroy the study of philosophy but would see it renewed and through its renewal give others the courage to philosophize themselves and not simply make imitative use of reason in the name of philosophy.

"Know Thyself!" But do not be afraid in the face of that revelation that leaves you naked before all the world. Do not long, philosopher, for the approval of any but reason and abandon the security of the institution as the only venue for the disclosure of your sacred thought. The names of a thousand reviewers and still a thousand more citations will not shield your words from the scrutiny of a logic in love with truth.

Why do I say all these things? Why am I being so painfully bare? Why explain my failure and success? Plainly, because very few philosophers ever explain themselves as human beings. It isn't proper. And yet, "Know thyself!" Any philosophy 101 course contains reference to this injunction. I allow exposure in the vain hope that someone, having seen me as a man, will listen to me as a thinker, and engage me honestly as a philosopher. I am not afraid of disagreement. Disagreement is simply part of the human condition. Ignorance frightens me, however, for in the actions of the ignorant are the seeds of injustice. There is often ignorance, especially among those who deal with philosophy professionally, of the fact that philosophers are human beings. We are so quick to toss names about, even designate whole schools of thought as Cartesian or Sartrean, that we take for granted the lives these people lived that inspired them to the heights of thought. We are so ready to assume that we have a handle on these people that we invoke merely their last names to solidify our own claims to truth. Leibniz will help here, why thank you, Nietzsche, for agreeing so amiably with my point. Let us not take each other for granted, utilizing each other in turn merely as means to our own ends; what an immoral way to philosophize.

How does one write about such things as freedom and the self without himself being free? How can we address the perennial questions if the course of our studies denies us the possibility of a return, if, as we make the round, we are chided, "No! Move forward, only forward! Say nothing unless it's new, the 'never-been-said' is your god!" Won't we then loose sight of the truths that stay with us, that are forever new because they are forever true? Won't we miss out on the opportunity to reformulate the true in terms compatible with our own times? I say these things because I am attempting to know myself, and, in my attempt, am hoping to show others it is okay to ask questions of and for themselves and to hold themselves accountable. Be not afraid that others may think you mad, or out of line, or a fool. Oh, to be young, people say, to live in the folly of youth! Look at me, address me, and do not dismiss me for my youthful follies.

"Know Thyself!" This is the theme most central to the task of this book. By way of introduction, I have explained all I need regarding my motivations for publishing this work. I have, perhaps inadvertently, also revealed very much about how I think philosophy ought to operate, and that there is a difference between studying philosophy (the history of philosophy) and doing philosophy, that is, philosophizing. The essays in this book came about from me being a student of philosophy and, as a student, learning how to philosophize.

The title essay of this volume is the longest. It consists of six parts, or Studies, and deals primarily with a theory of personal identity that is ethically grounded. In some ways, it argues that ethics is the first philosophy. Emmanuel Levinas, Albert Camus, and Luce Irigaray are primary influences, but I cannot ignore the work of Paul Ricoeur as being important to the overall understanding of my arguments here. The general thesis is that Otherness forms the ground of my identity, to the extent that I am Other to myself, and that my own Otherness is precisely the ground on which self-consciousness becomes possible. Ethical implications spring from the very roots of this thesis and are acknowledged throughout the essay as being of central importance to any plausible theory of the human person.

The brief "Interlude" is a meditation and exercise in free writing based on the work of Nietzsche. It uses Nietzsche's *Untimely Meditations* as a foil for a series of aphorisms that are themselves the subject of subsequent analysis. This literary exercise forms a key example of the philosopher struggling to know himself before the public eye and through the medium of his own philosophical writings.

The second longest essay of the current work follows the "Interlude." "The Freedom of Action" deals primary with an argument for how the self, as detailed in "The Ontological I," is both free and morally responsible. It builds on the themes of the title essay while elaborating at length on the functions of consciousness and perception in free actions that take place in a deterministic world.

"The Subject in Rebellion" is the oldest essay presented here, and expands greatly on the roles that negation and rebellion play in personal identity, and thereby in moral responsibility as well. It deals with themes introduced in the Fourth, Fifth, and Concluding Studies of "The Ontological I" while focusing much more tightly on the specific roles of objectification and rebellion against objectification in the formation of a personal identity.

The film *Black Swan* is the subject of philosophical analysis in "Nihilism and Archetype." This short essay was originally published on my blog and serves as a bridge between the strictly academic aspects of this volume and the pop culture in which each person struggles to form an idea of themselves among the others with whom that culture is shared, amongst whom it is "popular" culture. It explores the formation of identity and the consequences of self-deception and dissociation that occur in the film.

The final essay presented here, "The Free Spirit Parallax," deals primarily with the philosophical writings of Nietzsche on the topic of the "Free Spirit." I counter commentary on Nietzsche's theories that attempt to systematize and objectify Nietzsche's thought. I also draw from Nietzsche's text the idea that struggle is central to freedom, and that it is only through a struggle against our own internal contradictions that we ourselves may become free.

Each essay deals with personal identity, and as such, each is concerned with the self, the soul, or the will. Sometimes, these terms are interchangeable (often "I," "self," or "soul" are used interchangeably). In other instances, context demands strict definitions (in these instances I use more specific terms, such as "agent" or "subject") but in all cases, the most general sense of these terms is just this: the living human person as they are capable of functioning autonomously in the world, i.e. a conscious person, aware of themselves as such. Thus we get the title of the volume *The Ontological I*, the I that is capable of ontology, of thinking and questioning in regards to that being's own being.

Readers will notice that some of the essays ("Interlude" and "Nihilism and Archetype") have little or no citation. Other essays are extensively annotated with both academic citation and notes of explanatory or exegetical functions. Citation does nothing to strengthen an argument beyond lending examples of agreement. The purpose of citation, in this volume, is to reflect agreement or disagreement with other philosophers, and to situate the current work within a certain body of similar works, all of which I have read and which have contributed (both positively and negatively) to the expression of my own views in some way. As such, citation here serves a strictly literary function. The literary function of the citation is simply an organizational one. It helps to establish a certain axiology among the ideas presented here, notes being digressions from the main arguments or detours through the thinking of other writers. Occasionally, a note will be used for exegesis, in the hope that further explanation will make the point appear more clearly, though such extra emphasis is really not essential to the work as a whole. As endnotes, all notes appear at the end of each section, not at the end of the entire volume. This was done for ease of reference without unnecessarily weighing down each page with excessive notation and reference. Chicago style endnotes were utilized for their clarity, and for their unobtrusive appearance in the text itself.

It may seem strange that I make such explicit reference to the formal organizational aspects of this book as a physical object, that is, as a manuscript, a book one will read as an activity. Again, I do so because philosophers rarely, if ever, do this We take the form of the book for granted. We throw citation at the end of the sentence as if this practice were clear to everyone, as if each person knows intuitively the functions of each note, of each reference, as if we could be lead through the superscript to the author. But this detour to the other philosopher only brings more detours to still other philosophers in the work of the first other. Philosophizing will always be, to some degree, a systematizing activity. We are concerning ourselves with expressing and explaining a coherent world—even when we sometimes insist on its incoherency or chaos. The idea that the world is incoherent makes sense of the world; it remains a unifying concept, a principle under which we organize the world incoherently. A theory of incoherency is still expected to be logically coherent. To the reader, then, citations are contextualizing tools, conduits into a system of the history of philosophy that, by referring the reader to other authors, allows certain interpretational tools to be recommended by implication.

The reference can be at once an endorsement and a refutation. Read this, but read it and agree or disagree. The reference situates us toward the work of others. From it, the current work implicitly takes its stance. Thus, in citation the author often reveals prejudice. Interesting how the supposed instrument of objectivity here becomes a double sword in which the subjectivity of the author is revealed. For the reference can only refer to that which the author has read, thus only to the choice of the author, an account of the author's reading habits. But here too a great joy in the possibility of a dialogue. Even the opening to correspondence.

Citation is also a confession of the desire for a shared identity—a binding agreement between us that enables a delineation of the terms of inquiry. Thus, method, pedagogy, the meta-level analysis that allows us to ask together "what is the proper way to proceed?" I am not alone in my studies, and I signal the community to join in my work by sending up the flag of the endnote to signal that here we draw inspiration from one another. It is also an indication of seriousness. That I take this business seriously and have taken others seriously and give them credit for the work they undertook and the achievements in thought they've made, even when, or especially when, I'm in disagreement with one or more of those works. It is a way of seeking acceptance, providing a criterion for judgment, the linguistic proof, a symbolic relic from the work that was done in the writing of the text. Strange that the work itself is not considered such a relic, but again, it is just to give credit where credit is due. Credit can be given in many forms.

This giving of credit is a form of responsibility. Again, the thematics of the work itself are reinforced even in the meta-analysis of work. Citation implies the question "Who is responsible?" The citation has already answered, "I and the other, for I wrote the words and the other was my inspiration." The author doesn't have to stand alone. But she might. I find myself in good company. The chorus of philosophy is a thousand voices deep.

However, this book is not about those voices. When I was preparing to defend my thesis, people at conferences and in seminars would ask me, "Who is your thesis on?" I thought this was a rather inappropriate question at first, but then the question was repeated with such frequency that I thought it might be I who was strange for questioning its propriety. I originally thought the question inappropriate because I was convinced one's thesis should be about a problem, or the proposal of a theory that explains some phenomena or prescribes a course of action etc. In other words, the thesis was about the author's ideas. But I was naïve. Of course, many scholarly people are so infatuated with the work of one particular thinker that they do work only on the work of the object of their infatuation. Sometimes, the stronger of these types adapts the work of their infatuation to other problems. We have nice linguistic tricks for this distinction, for instance one studies Kant, or does work on Kant, while the other is a Kantian, or has a Kantian theory of... I do work on Nietzsche, Kant, Camus, and many others. I have theories that could be described as Kantian, Aristotelian, Nietzschean, and I suppose other ways as well, phenomenological, hermeneutic and so on. Suppose then, I still find the question "Who is your thesis on?" to be inappropriate. As to what my theses are, I provided a brief abstract of each essay above and will repeat them again many times throughout my argumentation.

One thing that concerns me is clarity. I hope to be clear for my readers. Does this mean I have erased all ambiguity and rendered all my logic in perfect analyticity? —certainly not. I have never attempted such a task. But I have attempted, meticulously, to provide adequate roadmaps to point the way when the straightforward manner of writing fails to express my meaning. Metaphor plays a key role in the understanding of my work in general. If we appreciate the depth of metaphor, we will be prepared to deal with the three most difficult problems associated with the understanding of my philosophy. These three problems are: that my philosophy is atheistic, that my philosophy retains a religious tone, and that my philosophy contains a metaphysics of sorts not in fashion among today's intellectuals. Modern readers are sometimes confused to find me expounding and prescribing atheistic ideas in one instance and then turning to find an analysis of the Bible that treats the text as if there were profound truths to be found in its exegesis. It troubles some that I speak at length and favorably on St. Augustine and Nietzsche, Tolstoy and Bertrand Russell, Levinas and Camus. To those having difficulty understanding my intentions in doing this, I recommend you turn to the idea of metaphor for assistance.

Metaphor, most generally speaking, that is, metaphor as a figure of speech, is the application of a word or phrase to an object or concept to which that word or phrase is not literally applicable.

Thus, we have a secondary meaning: that the word or phrase is intended to act as a representative or as symbolic of something else, of some other, especially something abstract. Metaphysics is abstract. We see an obvious linguistic connection here.

For instance, take St. Augustine and Nietzsche. Often, St. Augustine and Nietzsche speak on the same topics: freedom, the origin of morality, the human person, God and belief in God, etc. Now, we jump and take care how drastically different St. Augustine and Nietzsche are from one another: believer and non-believer, and so on. Then, we calm a bit upon recalling how drastically different were the times in which the two men lived. "How could Augustine not be Christian?" I've heard people explain. Nietzsche just heralds the crisis of consciousness experienced by modern man under the machinations of technological society etc. But do we then conclude there is nothing else? Let us be disinterested in the differences of men, just for a moment. What of the structure of their thought? Might there be some obscure agreement there? It is questions such as these that the daring purveyor of the history of philosophy must ask if any fresh insight is ever to be wrung from the continued study of the canon. Thus there must be a free exercise in the dialectics imposed upon the dead. It must be the practice, not the method that drives innovation in the approach to old books. The basic question driving all method of interpretation or exegesis is "what will I find?"

It is this basic conceptualization of philosophy as wonder and curiosity that is missing today while the chorus of philosophy prescribes it in a thousand voices. We must recognize the use of metaphor not as an invalid form of abstraction, but as the valid inference from analogy that hinges upon an equivalence of parts. When we strike upon the proper equivalence the whole rings in a harmony of truth with the rest of the chorus and the vague and general thread that links the whole of philosophy can be picked up at the happy intervals of time we call "history".

This is philosophy for optimists, for the free spirit, and for music lovers. The development of a philosophy still capable of speaking to the common in us all is a project of vital significance to our culture and politics. A philosophy that clears space for the others among whom each of us is ourselves the other is an ethics—a theory of justice. It is on and within ourselves that we lay the groundwork; establish metaphysics, of the freedom of justice and the freedom to live justly. To just live: a clarion call from the current work, still just one voice among many. The chorus of philosophy is a thousand voices deep.

Notes to the Introduction

[1] Albert Camus, *Notebooks 1942—1951*, trans. Justin O'Brien, (New York: Harvest/HBJ, 1978), 67.

[2] Immanuel Kant, *Logic*, trans. Robert S. Hartman & Wolfgang Schwarz, (New York: Dover Publications, Inc. 1988), 30.

PRELUDE

Does the scaffolding
of the chair
rise to meet me
or I to it?

How would I know?
How do I know?
Symbols and signs...

Thesis: a statement: a suggestion.
The absence of a sign to signal myself by;
I am not these signs signaling—
I am abundance :: We are the overflow

The economy of breath
    between one another
traffics symbols and signs like sand-dollars.
                      Aloof, in absentia, I give the sign,
Am presented by the sign
Am given over to this other for whom the sign represents

                                          But I am not there.
                I have absconded the sign.

See me,
                                        there in the distance,
seated on a chair.

Can I even sit in this chair?
Can this chair hold me
without being able to touch me?
With no ability to touch,
to reach out
to feel,
what is this holding that I now am?

Simply,
I am not this holding,
but am held,
lifted, vaulted, and made light.
This unbearable lightness,
beneath the heaviness of the world,
this history
:: We are…

     We are this history we are not yet in.

  This now is the history yet to come.
It is openness as books are,
The text, sign,
chronicles narrated…
The present given
only as a present accepted
from the past by the future
now past…
yet I am.

  This history that I am not yet in
is not my history,
It is my responsibility.

In this way I see the other,
not a sign,
but a face.

Irreducible it beckons me.
Incomprehensible, it demands,
it bequeaths, it betroths.

Can I walk by faith
when I see the face
face to face?
    But never as it really is…

                is not this sign.
                is not this face.

It is seated, here, in the chair that does not touch me.
That cannot touch me.
That holds but does not contain me.

        Cradled in the seat of meaning

                      I am absent,

and in this absence,
accounted for.
But I am not this sign.
    Wear is my face? but is   a mask :   : the sign .

THE ONTOLOGICAL I

First Study: Introduction to the Problem

I celebrate myself, and sing myself,
And what I shall assume you shall assume,
For every atom belonging to me as good belongs to you.[1]

AN ENCOUNTER ON A PRECIPICE

Walking up to a precipice, I am seized with a self-awareness that initiates my inquiry into the ontological I. From the vantage of the great height provided by the precipice, the only meaningful ontological question, for me at least, becomes the question of the I. It is a question that has not been adequately verbalized. In purely formal terms, for instance those used by Emmanuel Levinas, the question is framed in terms of totality and infinity.[2] Here, infinity indicates the Absolutely Other—that which breaks with the totality by exceeding it and laying always beyond it in an asymmetrical relation that does not permit the derivation of the infinite's definition from an antithetical description of the totality. Totality, therefore, is being as the same, a being revealed by war wherein the individual is given over to and acts as the bearer of a force that commands them without their knowledge, sacrificing the unity of their present to a future that will determine each individual's ultimate meaning. In the totality, the final act alone constitutes the meaning of a person's life—each is given as a pawn to the epic narrative of history. As such, I am obliged to attach a certain degree of violence to the idea of totality, and likewise, a degree of hospitality or openness to infinity.

In my own encounter on the precipice, I experience the ontological question, initially, as a silent question. The silent question, rather than being paradoxical, is really a question I ask of myself. It is not some question I pose, or oppose, to another within the totality. I ask it of myself in silence, to myself as to another in silence, and thus do not break into this silence with the historical weight of my words. My words, once verbalized, historicize. I treat my silence, however provisionally, as some pre-historical moment wherein I am invited to speak. To speak for myself, and, perhaps, for some other that is myself, or would be. I find my question, qua this silence, is not yet properly verbalized. Because the question of the I has yet to be adequately verbalized, the answer I give on the precipice is one given in response to a silence that invites me to speak. It is only later, after I proclaim myself to be, that the question becomes clear to me. When I answer this question with "I," or call out "Here I am!" and hear its cavernous refrain, I must admit that the floodgates of memory are opened and my being is then constituted in terms of history, in terms of how I came to be there on the precipice. The encounter with myself can be seen as a transitory suspense between forgetfulness and memory wherein I must forget myself in order to remember who I have become. The same tension between that magnitude of the infinite and the finitude of the finite are then played out in my own being as the tension between my determinate past and my indeterminate future, or, rather some future which I have yet to determine. Thus suspended in this transition, I find myself always in motion, always engaged in some movement both away from and towards myself. In a sense, I discover that I am mediated to myself by something other than myself. I become, in self-recognition, other to myself in order to apprehend what I myself am. This forms the thesis of the current work: that I am mediated by Otherness. What is meant by this "Otherness" will be developed as we proceed. For now, we must remain obscure, and work toward a deeper understanding through philosophic analysis.

THE PHENOMENOLOGAL APPROACH

My home in the Appalachian Mountains is but a gentle succession of these high vantages upon which the driftwood of Western civilization has come to a comfortable repose. Living among these mountains heaped and piled in mounds around the highest of their peaks I developed a taste for great heights and the vantage they provided, but always noted that this desirability arose from a peculiar tension between my own smallness and the greatness of a vast expanse of land stretching out into a misty dawn.

Here, where mining has created plateaus upon which the expanse opens on all sides, where the high flat mountain sinks into itself, and the wind creates an atmosphere of ever-shifting sensations, the "I" appears on the precipice as the locus of an immanent and indeterminate horizon. Standing upon the leveled plane, the hollow mountain languishing beneath me in the sun, the tension between limitation and limitlessness becomes visceral and constitutes the phenomenological manifestation of the ontological I. The interplay of the determinate being with its indeterminate environment underscores an attempt to be on the precipice *in the moment*. Focusing my attention on the present in order to have an experience on the precipice pantomimes the theoretical bracketing of considerations exterior to the phenomenon of the vantage. Though my history may have led me to the precipice, I attempt to forget it in order to engage the vantage from the precipice as it is. Again, there is tension between the limitations of the historical past, the facticity of what has happened prior and the possibilities invoked by a perspective that outstrips that facticity.[3]

The phenomenological credo, originating with Hegel[4] and carried by Husserl[5] into the twentieth century, is, as I interpret it, "to the things themselves!"[6] With our focus drawn in this way to my encounter on the precipice *as I experience it* we are in a position to carry out a Husserlian "bracketing" of all theoretical knowledge not immediately pertinent to the experience had on the precipice. What I undergo, in order to "be in the moment," is an active forgetting of my experiences exterior to the encounter itself.

However, this activity of forgetting myself for a moment is only temporary, and, when the brackets are removed, I am in a situation to become critical, from the perspective gained from my encounter on the precipice, of what had been bracketed. As such, phenomenology is only a first step in the inquiry. When I make the critical move, from the experiential emphasis of phenomenology to the theoretical emphasis of self-reflection, I am making a move to hermeneutics. On this point I do not want to conflate critique and hermeneutics, they are not identical. However, I do want to suggest that hermeneutics is the first step toward critique for the reason that it opens the question, or often, reopens the question. My understanding of the role of hermeneutics diverges from Hans Georg Gadamer on this point and aligns more closely with Paul Ricoeur, specifically, the idea of hermeneutics laid out in his essay, "The Problem of Double Meaning as Hermeneutic Problem and as Semantic Problem." There he asks if it is not philosophy's task to "ceaselessly reopen, toward the being which is expressed, this discourse which linguistics, due to its method, never ceases to confine within the closed universe of signs and within the purely internal play of their mutual relations?"[7] Methodologically speaking, the current work could be classified as an exercise in hermeneutic phenomenology.

HERMENEUTIC PHENOMENOLOGY

The relation of the ontological I to itself is the relation of an inquirer who inquires into the being of the inquirer. It creates, superficially at least, a hermeneutic circle wherein the inquiry leads simultaneously away from and toward the object of inquiry. It is led toward itself by itself, or is led away from itself by itself. Is this an insurmountable paradox?

The short answer is "no," as the aim of hermeneutics is to overcome just such an obstacle. Gadamer describes the hermeneutic circle to the effect that: "It is not so much our judgments as it is our prejudices that constitute our being."[8] He elaborates that, "The nature of the hermeneutical experience is not that something is outside and desires admission. Rather, we are possessed by something and precisely by means of it we are opened up for the new, the different, the true."[9] It is these prejudices that I have attempted to bracket on the precipice. Specifically, I want to forget the historical aspect of my being from which I derive cultural prejudices or socialized ways of responding to the world. Note that I use the word prejudice in much the same way Gadamer does and this use does not indicate the purely negative prejudice associated with racism, sexism, or anti-Semitism. I rather use prejudice in the simple manner found in Nietzsche, as a way to talk about those things we assume to be the case without reflection or criticism.

In the phenomenology of the precipice I attempt to be as I am in myself, just one entity in the world. I am not *essentially* this entity in the world; my description is of a relation of myself opening up unto the world. This opening up is described in the movement into the critical mode of hermeneutics wherein I reflect upon the prejudices that I had actively forgotten. I now recall those from the critical stance and attempt to analyze these prejudices according to the relations described on the precipice. I am undertaking an essentially ontological project by turning the hermeneutic analysis on myself in this way. I have made myself into a problem.

Here we see Heidegger's influence on someone like Gadamer or myself. When we read a passage such as, "The ontic distinction of Existence lies in the fact that it is ontological,"[10] the ontic suggests a characteristic of being, an aspect that is taken on or embodied by being. Here we translate *Auszeichnung* as "distinction" because it smacks of Honor, of being "signed or signified (*zeichnung*) out (*Aus*)" and thus of being set apart, made special and unique in a particular way. The distinction is a special mark—we may even say a commemoration—of the Heideggerian *Dasein* that I translate simply as "Existence." But there is a strong connection in our analysis to the literalness of translating *Dasein* as "There-being" because of the contextualization of the precipice. We are *there*, on the precipice, and it is this specificity that creates the distinction of being ontological. Thus, the encounter on the precipice is an encounter with myself, with the self. It is through the relation we maintain with the horizon that our own being becomes a problem for us.

My relation to the horizon that opens before me defines me. To be clear, I am opening up to the world, as I have said, but I am not opening unto a world that is closed to me. Rather, I am opening, as if from an enclosure, unto openness. More precisely, my opening denotes the openness of the world in general. The meaning of the latter will come into sharper relief as we elaborate on the fact that we are always already in the world, that I do not proceed as if from the interior of myself into the world. The closure of which I speak is properly understood as the *past*. We have focused here on the horizon whose metaphor informs our discourse. The openness of the horizon designates a relation of possibility. The limit of the vantage is indeterminate. The earth is taken over by the sky at some point where the two seem to meet but do not. The optical effect is the dissemination of the limitations into themselves, earth and sky, sky and earth. The fact of the earth's roughly spherical dimensions only reinforces this intuition when we see the earth falling perpetually away from the sky, thus into itself in virtue of its approximate circularity. The sky does not offer this perspective because, rather than intimating a totality, as the closed, spherically pointillistic manifestation that the appearance of the earth in space implies, its openness points us toward the infinite. I need not belabor us with the scientific metaphor of the vastness of space to make this point clear.

What is the sky if not the gradual dissemination of the Earth's density into a vast expanse? The earth is given over to the expanse as I am given over to the horizon. My vision, linked with conscious perception, the historic touchstone of selfhood, fails when it confronts this horizon and in this failure to capture the expanse within a totalizing view reveals me in my finitude. But I feel myself disseminating into the expanse of this horizon. This is the horizon's openness to me. I feel at once an invitation but also a refusal. I am kept at this distance from the horizon regardless of how I change my perspective on the precipice. This distance maintains me in my relation to the horizon. From this relation comes the question with which I answer "I am." Interiority denotes this separation of myself from the horizon; the silence is non-affectational separation to which affectation is me reaching out *as if to myself*.

ONESELF IN THE WORLD

Allow me, in order to elucidate how I wish to answer the aforementioned question, to fill in my encounter on the precipice with some detail as to what I see myself in relation to. That is, of what does this landscape consist? What constitutes that expanse that fades into an indeterminate horizon? What invites me to the encounter with myself?

When I look over many of the vistas a great vantage in the Appalachians provides, there are very often small towns and communities dappling the curvature of the landscape with elements of human culture. No feature speaks more prominently of this than the church steeple. It is most likely that for every center of human activity nestled in the landscape there is at least one steeple, and often there are many more. There may be other landscapes wherein the activity of human life is expressed in a different manner. Perhaps an urban setting would further emphasize technology, or the economic aspect of the human landscape. But in the rural landscape, I find, it is the steeple.

When this irredeemably human symbol is seen from this great height, the moment I attempt to engage in becomes reflective. The steeple draws me to the transcendent by its form. It points skyward, toward what I had already designated as a metaphoric infinite. More importantly, it points skyward with historical authority. No matter what I may forget while engaging the horizon from the precipice, I cannot pretend that each steeple is not founded on a church. I cannot get far enough away to forget a church is a church. Likewise, I cannot forget that a silo is a silo, a billboard is a billboard, and power lines are power lines. These are marks of the human and as such indict me.

For instance, when I see the church I must decide what I am to do with God. After all, God had been bracketed in my attempt to be in the moment. I had forgotten God. But seeing His house in the foothills of Appalachia brings God into the moment with me and forces me to decide what relation I am to take to Him. The transcendent also appears on the horizon in this way. The steeple denotes an aspect of the landscape that speaks to me in terms I can readily understand. However, if the vantage is sufficiently high, or atheism again casts God from the relation, the meaningfulness of one space becomes lost in the excess of the expanse surrounding it. The absurd feeling begins to set in. The comparison is invoked. The church is supposed to represent Absolute authority; it is an earthly symbol of God's authority, more importantly it is a *human* symbol of God's authority. How easily that significance has been undermined by the simple elegance of a very large space. Doubt has been writ large. From the vantage of a great height, the human meaning that calls back to me from the landscape begins to loose its urgency and the Absolute, as expressed in the human, is dissolved in a magnitude that can only be indifferent to the finitude of the human. It is not only God, but also anything that we may perceive to be Absolute, from science to the economy; what good will physics be when that which it explained has dissipated into entropy? Here we arrive with Albert Camus at the absurd reasoning.

ABSURDITY AND THE ONTOLOGICAL I

It is this absurdity of modernity from which Camus makes his philosophic start.[11] He writes, "The feeling of the absurd is not, for all that, the notion of the absurd. It lays the foundations for it and that is all."[12] Thus, my feeling of the absurd on the precipice is not to be confused with the Absurd itself, which "springs from a comparison…bursts from the comparison of a bare fact and a certain reality, between an action and the world that transcends it."[13] The absurd is not in myself, nor in something exterior to myself, but in the presence of the two together. The relational character of myself to the horizon awakens me to the feeling of the absurd. It is not that I am myself Absurd, nor is it that the world is itself Absurd. Rather, I render myself absurd through my reasoning about myself as an entity in the world, specifically in a world that is described as indifferent to me. For me, the Absurd denotes a fundamental problematization of myself wherein my very being becomes essentially absurd by comparison to an indifferent objective world. Casual or artistic absurdity must be differentiated because it is merely a way of thinking, a contrivance based solely on our own judgment regarding, and this is key, *a particular situation*. We will see how this can be turned into a positive manifestation, but here, on the precipice, it is an *unsettling* feeling. I am *de-centered*, and alienated from the landscape.

Admittedly, the Absurd is a specifically historical phenomenon. The interesting thing about the history of absurdity is that it manifests itself predominantly from the atheistic perspective—such as in modernity, but also in a peculiar fashion among the Greeks, who were of course the original atheists. As atheism has a strange and negative connotation in the contemporary ear, I want to point to it as a theme of this thesis that will undergo considerable metamorphosis as we progress. There is theism, in one sense among the Greeks. But it is only from the perspective of Christianity that atheism takes on the meanings associated with it today. For the early Christians, the Greeks, among many others, were *essentially* atheists, that is, they believed falsely about God: the Grecian view of the gods is without God. What other impetus for conversion? So we have, on one hand, the Absurd character of the "human condition" as formulated by the existentialists. On the other hand, we have absurdity as manifest in the story of Œdepis Rex wherein the absurd outcome of the story is ordained by the gods,[14] and the absurd relation itself fulfills a divine teleology. We see this ordination of absurdity in the Old Testament, for instance in the story of Job's persecution, which has instigated atheistic critiques.

However, I do not wish to endorse this Absurd outlook. Rather, I wish to combat it (as Camus did) as one would combat the encroaching symptoms of an epidemic. In our age, Absurdity is the epidemic of the spirit that tells us we are nothing, we are the products of chance, and as such ought to despair at the essential meaninglessness of our lives. I offer this excerpt from Bertrand Russell as an example of Absurd logic at its finest and most difficult to combat. He writes,

> That man is the product of causes which had no prevision of the end they were achieving; that his origin, his growth, his hopes and fears, his loves and his beliefs, are but the outcome of accidental

> collocations of atoms; that no fire, no heroism, no intensity of thought and feeling, can preserve an individual life beyond the grave; that all the labors of the ages, all the devotion, all the inspiration, all the noonday brightness of human genius, are destined to extinction in the vast death of the solar system, and that the whole temple of man's achievement must inevitably be buried beneath the debris of a universe in ruins—all these things, if not quite beyond dispute, are yet so nearly certain that no philosophy which rejects them can hope to stand. Only within the scaffolding of these truths, only on the firm foundation of unyielding despair, can the soul's habitation henceforth be safely built.[15]

Quite a tall order, but worthy of Tolstoy's lament, "Now I cannot help seeing the days and nights rushing toward me and leading me to death. I see only this, and this alone is truth. All else is a lie."[16] Now the "I" has become truly problematic. The ontological question is most fully revealed, as Tolstoy intimates to us that "The horror of the darkness was too great, and I wanted to be free of it as quickly as possible by means of a rope or a bullet. It was this feeling, more powerful than any other, that was leading me toward suicide."[17]

These passages speak directly to the problem of being as I have outlined it. But is this the conclusion that we must draw? I argue it is not. Further, I will attempt to show how the way beyond Absurdity is contained within the thinking of the Absurd itself, so that thereby even those dwelling with the conviction of Absurdity may find their way to an affirmation of themselves. In a sense, I wish to show how I found my own way out of Absurdity. The way out, as I see it, is through a critical examination of the history of the theoretical self as it is imparted through Western culture. I must be critical of the Self as I see it already in the world, such as in the church whose steeple beckons to me from the precipice, or as it is displayed upon billboards that illuminate a cityscape with enticements to a materialistically construed happiness. In short, I must undertake the critical examination of the prejudices with which I already see myself. I will see in what ways I am mediated to myself as being always already in the world. Thus, I will demonstrate the ways in which I am other to myself. In this Otherness, which is yet to be expounded upon, we find a fundamental aporia that will form the basis of the following study.

At this juncture, we see that the current work is one of philosophic anthropology. Ricoeur suggests this moved toward philosophical anthropology in his early work, *Fallible Man*. We shall see if we discover with him the germ of the transcendent in the relation between "openness and perspective."[18] The transcendental aspect of phenomenology is likely unavoidable given the power of Husserl's influence in twentieth century philosophy. A philosophical anthropology at first seems antithetical to the transcendent because the transcendent is a formal formulation. Only an *active* transcendent would be pertinent to a philosophical anthropology: a *metanthrōpos*.

RECAPITULATION

Husserl himself praised philosophical anthropology by saying:

> Initially, phenomenology, conceived as transcendental doctrine, refused to derive any part of the foundations of philosophy from any science of man and opposed, as "anthropologism" and "psychologism," all attempts in this direction. But now, on the contrary, one looks to human existence as the sole basis for the reconstruction of phenomenological philosophy.[19]

In the current study, we see philosophical anthropology arising very naturally from hermeneutic phenomenology. This constitutes the overall methodological approach of the current work. Through these methods I will demonstrate how the I is mediated, specifically, how it is mediated through Otherness. In some ways, we shall see how I am other to myself. We derive the phenomenological aspect of the inquiry from my encounter on a precipice. We will be referred to the precipice thematically throughout the subsequent studies. This contextualization will provide a foundation from which my hermeneutic analysis may begin. Through such an analysis I hope to indict the prejudices with which I currently judge myself and attain a radically different understanding of myself, and the Self in general. This is the philosophic project we are currently engaged in. As it stands, history will play a large role in the subsequent studies, both in the sense of the history of philosophy and in my own personal history. It is from the history of philosophy that I inherit my prejudices, and it is my own personal history that is now to be cleansed of these prejudices. Once reconstituted thusly, I hope to find myself safely beyond the logic of the Absurd, my feet firmly planted on a plane made level by philosophic reflection.

COMMENCING FROM THE ORIGIN

The following study will deal with aporia. This aporia is the result of the history of philosophy. It is only through the uncritical maintenance of this aporia that the Absurd logic arises. Therefore, if the Absurd is to be cast out, we must address the heart of the aporia itself without blindly maintaining the structure it recommends. As we see the aporia arising from the history of philosophy, it is perhaps most difficult for us to see the aporetic structures most near to us historically. I will therefore begin much earlier in history and attempt to outline an origin from whence the aporia proceeds.

By doing so we do not condemn the study to fall to the genetic fallacy.[20] The origin does not determine the I to be what it is in itself. Instead, I want us to see how the I has been set-up for us conceptually. In the above sections I described a process through which the I, or at least myself, becomes reflective. Reflection occurs in a critical mode as it is described above and the purpose of this reflection is to attain a deeper and more nuanced understanding of the I. Thus, we will commence the inquiry from the origin in the hopes of seeing the development of the aporia as it proceeds from one formulation to the next.

Notes to the First Study

[1] Walt Whitman, "Song of Myself." *Leaves of Grass*, (New York: Bantam Books, 1983), 22.

[2] When speaking from the purely formal perspective (the impersonal perspective) I myself will refer to totality and infinity as Levinas defines these terms. See *Totality and Infinity*, trans. Alphonso Lingis, (Pittsburgh: Duquesne University Press, 1969); 21, 26—7.

[3] Jean-Paul Sartre deals with this at length in *Being and Nothingness*, trans. Hazel E. Barnes (New York: Washington Square Press, 1992); 619—707. The theme of the individual's relation to the historical community is also a theme, perhaps the dominant theme, of Sartre's *Critique of Dialectical Reason, vol. 1*, trans. Alan Sheridan-Smith, (New York: Verso, 2004).

[4] Who writes, "our approach to the object must also [like knowledge] be *immediate* or *receptive*; we must alter nothing in the object as it presents itself." *Phenomenology of Spirit*, trans. A. V. Miller, (Oxford: Oxford University Press, 1977), 58.

[5] Who writes, "...phenomenology does nothing but interrogate just that world which is, at all times, the real world for us; the only one which is valid for us, which demonstrates its validity to us; the only one which has any meaning for us." See "Phenomenology and Anthropology." Trans. Richard G. Schmitt, *Realism and the Background of Phenomenology*, ed. Roderick Chisholm, (Glencoe: The Free Press, 1960), 142.

[6] An interpretation I share with Martin Heidegger, *Being and Time*, trans. John MacQuarrie & Edward Robinson, (New York: Harper & Row, 1962), 50.

[7] Paul Ricoeur, "The Problem of Double Meaning as Hermeneutic Problem and as Semantic Problem." *The Conflict of Interpretations*, trans. Kathleen McLaughlin, (Evanston, IL: Northwestern university Press, 1974); 62—78.

[8] "The Universality of the Hermeneutical Problem." *Philosophical Hermeneutics*, trans. David E. Linge, (Berkeley: university of California Press, 1977), 9.

[9] Ibid, 9.

[10] *Die ontische Auszeichnung des Daseins liegt darin, daß es ontologisch ist.* Martin Heidegger, *Sein und Zeit*. (Tübingen: Max Niemeyer, 1967), 12.

[11] *The Myth of Sisyphus* begins, as does much philosophy, with some discourse on the history of ideas, treating Husserl and Heidegger, among others. Albert Camus, *The Myth of Sisyphus*, trans. Justin O'Brien, (New York: Vintage International, 1991); 10—28. We cannot avoid the constant presence of Sartre in Camus thinking, much as Hume shadows Kant's *Critiques*.

[12] Ibid, 28.

[13] Ibid, 30.

[14] Of course, Œdepis unwittingly slays his father and marries his mother, thus bringing his kingdom to ruin, just as the gods had determined. However, the consummation of Œdepis' fate does not absolve him and he suffers greatly from his realization, *from the comparison he draws between what he believes to be the case and what actually is the case*, and he gouges out his own eyes before fleeing into self-imposed exile. See Sophocles, *The Oedipus Tyrannus of Sophocles*, trans. Sir Richard Jebb, (Cambridge: Cambridge University Press, 1887).

[15] Bertrand Russell, "A Free Man's Worship." *Why I Am Not a Christian and Other Essays on Religion and Related Subjects*, (New York: Simon & Schuster, 1957), 107.

[16] Leo Tolstoy, *Confession*, trans. David Patterson, (New York: W. W. Norton & Co, 1996), 31.

[17] Ibid, 33.

[18] Paul Ricoeur, *Fallible Man*, trans. Charles A. Kelbley, (New York: Fordham University Press, 1986); 46, 24.

[19] Husserl, "Phenomenology and Anthropology," 129.

[20] As outlined in: Morris Cohen & Ernest Nagel, *An Introduction to Logic and Scientific Method*, (New York: Harcourt, Brace & World, 1934); 388—89.

Second Study: Aporetic Origins

Of ways you may speak,
    But not the Perennial Way;
By names you may name,
    But not the Perennial Name.[1]

IN THE BEGINNING, THERE WAS DIFFERENCE

In the previous study, I had indicated the church as one source of my prejudices regarding myself. I should clarify what I mean when I use the word "prejudice." I mean precisely those judgments that I assume to be the case. They are pre-reflective, those prejudices of philosophers whose values color my perception of the landscape. The hermeneutical aspect of this phenomenology must, therefore, call into question the "things themselves" toward which Heidegger would direct his analysis if we are to reopen the question of the I beyond its being, beyond its identity as being always the same being—thus adapt a Nietzschean avarice to the assumption that:

> ...the things of the highest value must have another, peculiar origin—they cannot be derived from this transitory, seductive, deceptive, paltry world, from this turmoil of delusion and lust. Rather from the lap of Being, the intransitory, the hidden god, the 'thing-in-itself'—there must be their basis, and nowhere else.[2]

The steeple had spoken to me from the landscape about myself and indicated to me the humanity in an inhuman landscape. It also instigated the feeling of the Absurd. It is the first historical landmark from which I will attempt to trace the original aporia of my own being, of the being of the I. Before I engage what is admittedly a cursory historical overview, I want to caution my readers against the assumption that I am making a case for something like the "correct" historical theory of identity. First, I am given the interpretation of the history of philosophy as I see it; that is, as it has contributed to my own philosophical prejudices. Secondly, I am attempting to trace, not the theory of selfhood, but the aporia upon which divergent theories revolve. Largely, this central aporia can be described in terms of embodiment, by what has traditionally been termed the "Mind/Body" problem. It is not my concern to resolve this problem; it has been formulated so as to be non-resolvable. Rather, I will show how this central division informs the conceptual history of the self even where theorist differ drastically from one another. Let us, therefore, commence our studies with a consideration of the Creation of Man as the Bible[3] gives it to us. In this way, I introduce an account of the origin of the self that is historically rooted, and this historicity lends the Creation of Man its narrative structure. The Creation is existentially significant as an interpretive structure—that is, the world of The Creation provides a basis for acting a certain way.

From the outset, it is necessary to note that the Creation of Man is inextricably bound to the Myth of the Fall. There is an immanent sense in which the actual creation of man is the Fall, not the Adamic creation story. However, we will see how the two function together to account for the origin of the I as it is understood from the Judeo-Christian perspective.

Following the initial creation story is a second account that proceeds in varying details from the first. The creation of man is presented in a passage that reads, "Then the Lord God formed a man from the dust of the ground and breathed into his nostrils the breath of life. Thus the man became a living creature." (Gen, 2:7) The word man is used here in a general sense and translates the Hebrew word *adam*; the man in question is not yet named. He is merely a "living creature." The breath of God is shown to animate dumb matter. The earth itself is gathered up, given form, and then brought to life by the infusion of God's breath. The Hebrew word *adamah* is given here as "dust of the ground," providing an intimate connection between what is named "man" and that which he is composed. So too do we have a connection between the body and pure material being, and a connection between the spirit, or of the animating force of life, and God.

Of course, there is also the creation of the Tree of the Knowledge of Good and Evil and the injunction not to eat from that tree. (Gen, 2:9; 2:16) This injunction is issued with a warning that "for on that day that you eat from it, you will certainly die."

(Gen, 2:17) Note the moral imperative is delivered prior to the creation of the woman from man's rib in Genesis 2:21—4. So far, Genesis 2 has recast the story of creation as a set up for the fall. The entire narrative movement of creation in the second account culminates in the foreshadowing of the very shame man and wife will feel upon eating the forbidden fruit. (Gen, 2:25) Shame is already present; man and woman simply do not realize it yet—this is the narrative thrust of the story, the double assertion of humanity's ignorance and impending awakening is structured beforehand in the telling of the myth. They have no conscience, or are not conscious. They are living creatures but not yet human. The serpent is the vehicle by which the woman is tempted to that which will bring shame forth. He is the instrument of doubt, but also, the trigger for humanity's awakened conscience. So we may read "conscience," even "consciousness" as "self-doubt."

The serpent instigates doubt while at the same time making a promise of power. The woman confesses God's warning about the forbidden fruit to the serpent who tells her, "Of course you will not die. God knows that as soon as you eat your eyes will be opened and you will be like gods knowing both good and evil." (Gen, 3:3—5) The serpent contradicts God's word while at the same time offering a means by which to attain god-like knowledge, which is knowledge of shame, a specific construct of the more general knowledge of Good and Evil. The woman succumbs to the temptation, she takes the fruit to the man who also eats, and the couple realizes they are naked. (Gen, 3:6—7) Shame is indicated only outwardly by making clothes out of fig leaves and then hiding when they "heard the sound of the Lord God walking in the garden at the time of the evening breeze." (Gen, 3:7—8)

Upon being discovered the man and woman confess to being naked and thus reveal their disobedience to God who goes on to make a pronouncement over the serpent, the woman, and the man. (Gen, 3:9—19) In the pronouncements of verses 14 through 19 God renders the verdict of the Fall. Here man is exiled from God. So begins a great metaphysical tradition. Even after eating the fruit, it is still the Word of God that constitutes the knowledge that defines the man and woman. This is knowledge of a series of divisions, which I shall sketch below. The goal of this study will be to show in what ways these divisions reinforce the aporetic structure of the Self throughout Western philosophy.

The first division is between all the descendents of the man and woman and the descendents of the serpent. God says to the serpent, "I will put enmity between you and the woman, between your brood and hers. They shall strike at your head, and you shall strike at their feet." Recall the serpent as the vehicle of temptation. The serpent had presented the object of desire and undermined the woman's resistance, who in turn undermined the man's resistance. The image of one striking at the head of another who is striking at the feet of the first is circular and presents the vehicle of desire as being struck at while at once striking back. What humanity strikes out after will strike back at humanity perpetually throughout the generations.

The second division is between man and woman. This division has already been presupposed throughout the gendered language of the biblical accounts, but here, the teleological description of the gendered terms is laid out. "You shall be eager for your husband, and he shall be your master," this is the woman's punishment, in addition to the labor of childbirth, and the burdens of the man to be heaped upon these as well.

The third division is between man and the world. The following passages recount God's proclamation to the man, the culminating verdict of the Fall in which man becomes mortal and fully aware of himself as such.

> ...accursed shall be the ground on your account. With labor you shall win your food from it all the days of your life...You shall gain your bread by the sweat of your brow until you return to the ground; for from it you were taken. Dust you are, to dust you shall return. (Gen, 3:20—1)

And so the man and his wife are exiled from the sublime presence of God. For the first time, the name Adam is given in reference to the man and Eve to the woman. They are displaced from their home, cast out into a world that is unfamiliar to them with knowledge that has destabilized them. Man and wife are determined against one another. Man is divided against the world, and against the temptations that exist for him in the world. Difference constitutes the very nature of mankind in this account of the beginning of history. The remainder of this study will expound upon original difference throughout the history of philosophy. In this way we shall see how the fundamental aporia has been constituted and reconstituted.

THE APORETIC ORIGIN

The primary aporia is exemplified by the problems of embodiment. Embodiment is perhaps the most concrete expression of the aporetic structure of the I. In the biblical account the body was created from dust and then the breath of God animated the body and called it to life. We know that Aristotle lived from 384 to 322 BCE. The Old Testament accounts were generated over a period of years between the twelfth and the second century BCE.[4] I make these historical notes only to put into perspective the course of these ideas in the West. It is important to see the coalescence of cultural histories, those of religion and philosophy, for they share claims on the essence of human kind.

Aristotle writes at length on the ψυχή (psuchē) describing it as "substance in the sense which corresponds to the account of the thing. That means that it is what it is to be for a body of the character just assigned."[5] (412^{b}10—2) For Aristotle, the essence (the what it is to be for a body of the character just assigned) of a living thing is to be perceptive, to have "the power of receiving into itself the sensible forms of things without the matter…" (424^{a}18—19) Above all, the sense of touch is vital to the soul of a living thing, for "without touch there can be no other sense, and the organ of touch cannot consist of earth or of any other single element." (453^{b}2—3) Thus, psuchē is always embodied for Aristotle; the body is imbued with psuchē that constitutes a vital principle in a literal sense of vitality, a life-bringing function empowering a body thus constituted. The metaphoric breath of God parallels the embodiment of psuchē. Further, as an embodiment, psuchē refers not only to what we moderns call "psychological" movements. Aristotle had a very robust conception of what this vital force meant for the body so animated by it, hence his emphasis on touch.

> That is why we can dismiss as unnecessary the question whether the soul and the body are one: it is as though we were to ask whether the wax and its shape are one, or generally the matter of a thing and that of which it is the matter. Unity has many senses (as many as 'is' has), but the proper one is that of actuality. (412^b5—9)

These words respond in key ways to the Platonic conception of the human soul in which Aristotle was schooled. When using the generalities "Platonic" and "Platonism," I generally agree with the analysis if Lloyd P. Gerson, who expressed the five core theses of Platonism to be: 1) The universe has a systematic unity; 2) The systematic unity is an explanatory hierarchy; 3) The divine constitutes an irreducible explanatory category; 4) The psychological constitutes an irreducible explanatory category; and 5) Persons belong to the systematic hierarchy and personal happiness consists in achieving a lost place in that hierarchy.[6] Plato (428-348BCE) lived during Aristotle's lifetime and was his teacher at the Academy. For Plato, the question of the Soul's relation to the body was not to be dismissed so easily. As we shall see, it provides us with a second and contradictory understanding of humanity's embodiment.

Plato describes a Socratic discussion of psuchē in the Cratylus dialogue.[7] Here again is repeated the connection to breath. Socrates says,

> I think that those who gave soul its name had something like this in mind. They thought that when the soul is present in the body, it causes it to live and gives it the power to breathe the air and be revitalized (anapsuchon), and that when this revitalization fails, the body dies and is finished. (399^d)

The followers of Euthyphro are then cited as demanding more of the definition for psuchē. (400^a) We are then led to consider that everything that lives and moves about does so by the sustenance of the soul. Having secured this concession from his interlocutor, Hermogenes, Socrates then moves to consider the Pre-Socratic philosopher Anaxagoras, who believes the whole of nature (phusis) to be sustained by psuchē. In *On the Soul*, Aristotle treats Anaxagoras in a similar way, writing, "…Anaxagoras…declares the moving cause of things to be soul," (404^{a}25) and then goes on to point to an ambiguity that "in many places he [Anaxagoras] tells us that the cause of beauty and order is thought, and elsewhere that it is the soul." (404^{b}1) This ambiguity is problematic because Anaxogoras maintains that all living things have soul while only humans, and then not even all humans, can think or be possessed of thought in the sense of intelligence. This brings Aristotle, and us, back to Plato and our now very central aporia.

The *Timaeus* dialogue is cited by Aristotle as proof that Plato agrees with the tradition treating thought as that which brings beauty and order. In *Timaeus*, Plato fashions the soul out of elements or principles thereby making things imbued with a soul into things that know or perceive. (404^{b}7—17) This marks the key dissention of Aristotle from Platonic thought. For it is on the grounds that the soul is essentially an intelligible phenomenon that Socrates proceeds to show the soul is separable from the body and indestructible or immortal. For Aristotle the soul is inseparable from the body. For Plato, the soul is essentially differentiated from the body and separable from it.

I pause here to note that we have entered into a twenty-three hundred year old discussion already in progress. I may take the biblical account as a starting point, but it is not the oldest text to discuss human nature, the nature of the Self, or of the I. It is generally agreed that the ancient prose *Upaniṣads* all date from the eighth and seventh centuries BCE (from 800BCE to 601BCE), thus pre-dating the historical biblical manuscripts of the Old Testament compiled in the last two centuries BCE.[8] There are many sections of the *Upaniṣads* elaborating at length upon the nature of the Self and Soul. I am not suggesting that the Vedic tradition carries on a discussion parallel to the Western tradition. I simply mean to show that we enter, with the Vedic tradition, yet another debate concerning the relation of the Self to the transcendent.

However, themes of difference are repeated and developed across divergent traditions and, though I am skeptical about any alleged parallelism between the ancient religious teachings of East and West, there is compelling comparative work on the ancient lineages of these respective traditions. For instance, John Bussanich suggests that:

> Orphic-Pythagorean teachings about the nature of the soul and its transmigration, purification, and divination, Parmenides on being, just to mention the most prominent, are embraced by Platonists as

revelatory truths and in certain instances are similar in context and function to the *Upaniṣadic* 'great sayings' or *mahāvākyas*, for example, 'not this, not this' or 'you are that.' Thus, the Orphic-Pythagorean tradition is analogous in some respects to Vedic *śruti*, at least for Platonists, though because of the decentralized nature of Greek religion as regards scriptures, authority, and doctrines, the teachings are treated more eclectically than in India.[9]

The concept of movement, of breath, of the relation of the Soul to the body all become complicated and conflated and, as a result, the fragmentation obscures the entity being thus described. Philosophically, it becomes difficult to separate where these concepts end and begin. Already we see an elaborate conceptual interconnection here at the "origin" of these concepts. Just as the man was already formed before the Fall, these philosophical concepts are already formed before we even begin to discuss their merits. We are deepening the importance of the aporia. With it thus originally instituted, I come to an impasse on my way to a direct elucidation of the I. To be clearer, I will move away from this discussion of ancient philosophy and move forward in the history of philosophy. Keep in mind the distinction that differentiates between Aristotle and Plato. The difference concerns the unity of the soul with the body: they are unified and inseparable for Aristotle, they are unified but separable for Plato.

THE PHILOSOPHIC AND THE RELIGIOUS

There is perhaps no better figure in the history of philosophy than St. Augustine for illustrating the transition from the above discussion of the I to the discussion carried on in the Modern Period (1600-1800 CE). Augustine lived from 354 to 430 CE and is thus historically situated to offer insight into the convergence of the Judeo-Christian tradition with the philosophic traditions of the Greeks and Mesopotamians. In an essay on the debates between Christian Theologists and pagan/Platonist philosophers, Jeremy M. Schott suggests that "Platonic and Christian 'schools' were, to borrow a term from Benedict Anderson, 'imagined communities' that depended on the constant and repeated negotiation of identity and difference."[10] Taken with the work of Gerson and Bussanich, the above reminds us to move forward with a historically nuanced view of this conceptual development, considering Massoretic, so-called from the Hebrew *massorah*, texts of the Old Testament had been compiled relatively close to Augustine's lifetime; by about the second century CE after the destruction of Jerusalem in CE 70.[11]

St. Augustine knew of Aristotelian philosophy. He writes, "And what did it profit me that, when I was scarcely twenty years old, a book of Aristotle's entitled *The Ten Categories* fell into my hands?"[12] The saint's estimation is that Aristotle did not profit him; it hindered him because he then comprehended everything he experienced as existing within the categories. From Aristotle, Augustine developed a philosophic prejudice. No wonder he was shaken to discover in Plato the method of doubt![13] Augustine refers to the "Academics" who were followers of Arcesilaus and Carneades, the founders of a skeptical tradition in the Platonic Academy of the third century BCE. They emphasized the suspense of judgment in the pursuit of truth and consented to nothing more than the probability of a conclusion. Augustine would have known of them through Cicero's *Academica* and directed the dialogue *Contra Academicos* to address the problems posed by such a view.

I had addressed in Aristotle an analogue between psuchē and the breath of God; both attempt to describe a vital force that animates what would otherwise be an un-living mass. The root ψυσ- (psus-) means breath or wind and from its counterpart ψυσο- (psuso-) we get "filled with [air or breath]". It takes no stretch of the imagination to connect psuso- to psuchē, to Aristotle's treatment of breath, and the entire Greek dialogue concerning the relation of phusis to psuchē I have also shown in what ways Aristotelian philosophy responds to Plato and the Pre-Socratics. Augustine, in turn, addresses the infusion of the breath of God into the man's body by way of allegorical reading, a method he had learned from St. Ambrose.

Regarding his education in this tradition of allegory, Augustine tells of Simplicianus, who was Ambrose's spiritual father, a great influence to both Ambrose and Augustine. Simplicianus congratulates Augustine that, as he puts it, "I had not fallen upon the writings of other philosophers, which were full of fallacies and deceit…whereas in the Platonists, at every turn, the pathway led to belief in God and his Word."[14] At this point Nietzsche again appears to my mind. He writes, "Gradually it has become clear to me what every great philosophy so far has been: namely, the personal confession of its author and a kind of involuntary and unconscious memoir; also that the moral (or immoral) intentions in every philosophy constituted the real germ of life from which the whole plant had grown."[15] I do not mention Nietzsche to slight Augustine, only to indicate that their insights were very much the same. Augustinian philosophy comes to us in the form of a Confession because Augustine embraces this personal aspect of philosophizing. As such, his concerns are much different from Aristotle, who instructed men how to live. Augustine's method of instruction would be different.

For instance, when he writes on Genesis 2:7, Augustine employs allegorical readings of the text beginning from a multiplicity of possible meanings derived from the biblical narrative. Augustine's treatment of the passage of the breath of God into man reads as follows:

> If at this point there was only body, we should understand that the soul was at this point joined to the body. Perhaps the soul had already been made, but was still in the mouth of God, that is, in his truth and wisdom. But it did not depart from there as if separated by places, when it was breathed forth. For God is not contained by place, but is present everywhere. Or perhaps the soul was made when God breathed the breath of life into the mud he has formed so that the breathing forth signifies God's activity by which he made the soul in man by the spirit of his power. If the man who had been made was already body and soul, sensation was added to the soul by the breath, when man was made a living soul—not that his breath was turned into the living soul, but it acted upon the living soul.[16]

Taken together, each view of the breath's relation to the body together form a larger view. The process of bringing these conflicting readings into dialogue with one another is an expression of Platonic dialectic and destabilizes the question so that Augustine can point us to a deeper, ethical insight. Aristotle had not been abandoned. In fact, Aristotelian thought helps Augustine to construct the different readings of the soul's relation to the body; the concept that "sensation was added to the soul by the breath" employs a very Aristotelian understanding of psuchē.

Like Aristotle, Augustine dismisses the question of the unity of the body and soul. In this, he is un-Platonic. However, when Augustine writes,

> Hence, we ought to understand this passage so that we do not take the words "He breathed into him the breath of life, and he became a living soul" to mean that a part, as it were, of the nature of God was turned into the soul of man. Thus we are not forced to say the nature of God is mutable.[17]

we see that he is adopting a Platonic ethical view, warning of the sin of Pride, and expounding on the infinite nature of God. There is a mystery to faith, to life, that "We walk by faith, so long as we believe that which we do not see, but sight will be ours when we see Him face to face, as He really is."[18] Since we cannot encapsulate the infinite of God into Aristotelian categories, we cannot answer these questions directly. The soul, as the divine breath of life, is more than a merely formal explanation of a body.

The method of doubt taught Augustine to turn inward toward a rationalistic epistemology wherein "there is no criterion for truth resident in the senses."[19] What was to be doubted was the world set up as a barrier and a scourge to him. Thus, he invokes the very passage in Genesis where God pronounces judgment on man. Genesis 3:18 is quoted and the labor from which man gains his bread is compared to the futile labor with which Augustine attempted to fit the infinite magnitude of God into Aristotle's finite totality of categories.[20] The Church Father could just have easily written what Nietzsche in fact does, "formerly, one believed in 'the soul' as one believed in grammar and the grammatical subject: one said 'I' is the condition, 'think' is the predicate and condition."[21] Augustine moves beyond the merely formal analysis of psuchē as "what it is to be for a body of the character just assigned." This is the totalizing view that repels the saint. Augustine demands the infinite. About the infinite, the most powerful human beings must still stop before the saint and ask. Nietszche may remark on the feminine tenderness and nobility of Augustine, but he then goes on to explore the power exerted by the saint, who is a "riddle of self-conquest and deliberate final renunciation."[22] Where Aristotle invests us with the immanence of psuchē, Augustine defers vitality to the Absolutely Other. Only the Divinity satisfies Augustinian Will to Power, but this Divinity is an excess of being that overflows any categorical classification.

What it is to be for the body of the character just assigned is to be a problem, or more precisely to be faced with the consequences of the Fall, of the infinite distance from God. The problem, formulated in this way, is how to live, how to sustain the soul in its divorce from the divine source of its being in the world? The knowledge of the fruit has proven to be knowledge that problematizes, that puzzles and befuddles. And then there is doubt; doubt that will undermine whatever humans display faith in.

IDENTITY OF MIND AND BODY; OR THAT I AM

Augustine was unsettled by this doubt, and from his displacement we must push forward to the consummation of the aporia seeded by the Greeks.

There is little question that the figure most identified with the method of doubt is René Descartes. In the spirit of St. Augustine, and of Nietzsche, I will attempt to paint a less dogmatic picture of Descartes than is normally depicted. I am interested in the all too human side of Descartes, the side that was worried by the problem of his own being, who was troubled by doubt, as Augustine was troubled. Descartes lived between 1596 and 1650 CE, a time that is very much an age in which Christianity defines European culture. By this time, Augustine's writings had become a central pillar of the church, and thus of European society, so much so that Augustine's theology had been formulated into Aristotelian terms by St. Thomas Aquinas who writes, "For what is supremely true is supremely being, as Aristotle had said in II Metaphysics."[23] This quotation alludes directly to the Aristotelian nature of the five arguments he puts forth. Aquinas, who lived from 1225 to 1274 CE, wishes to speak plainly, as Aristotle did, on the substance of God.

Thus, philosophy and religion had come full circle in their dialectic with one another, displaying a new form of specifically religious philosophy. In Descartes, we see an epistemological movement against Aristotle as Scholastics like Aquinas construe him. This alone shows how Descartes' Method of Doubt differs from that which shook Augustine to active contemplation. When I speak of irrationalism in Augustine, I am seeing past his epistemology to the metaphysical support upon which his rationality is founded. Irrationalism appears in Augustine when he approaches God. For God, the saint renounces even Reason because the essence of his philosophy as religious is proved in the infinity of God. Therefore, even rationality must break down at God, for He would exceed any rational limitation. Descartes adapts Augustine's epistemological rationalism in order to render a priori principles with certainty, and the I would necessarily provide a foundation for these a priori commitments. Thus arises the "idea of infinity."

How has philosophy directed us from a question concerning the relation of soul to body, a question of what "I" refers to, to the question of infinity? It is this movement as explained by Cartesian philosophy that sets the stage for the following study.

The fame of Descartes shines trough most clearly in the legacy of the cogito, which is essentially Mind.[24] The infinitive form of cogito from Latin means, "to think, ruminate, ponder, consider, plan." Thus, the conjugated cogito as a subject comes with the presupposition that it is an active subject, and this verb/noun function denotes a movement. If we recall the ambiguity of *ontologisch* in Heidegger's writing that was discussed in the previous study, we see that cogito is ambiguous in much the same way, that it is a subject (thought) that is itself thinking itself. Here is the Aristotelian core of the Cartesian subject. There is a famous Aristotelian locution that is expressed: *noesis noesis noesos* (thinking thinking thinking; or, thinking thinking thought). The Method of Doubt is really a method for dispelling doubt. Augustine dissolved it in faith, Descartes in reason itself. The

Rationalist hypothesis grows from that of Anaxagoras who writes, "Other things all contain a part of everything, but Mind is infinite and self-ruling, and is mixed with no Thing, but is alone by itself."[25] Here again, mind is connected, though much more directly than Cartesianism admits, with the infinite. It seems a root of the ontological I rests in the definition of its relation to a transcendent reality, to the world in which it belongs—and understanding all of the ways in which it belongs in the world.

Aristotelianism is about more than just grammar, and the importance of touch in the concluding sections of *On the Soul* proves this point. The teleological worldview focused on movement in order to describe the unfolding of a purpose over time. The biblical narrative is likewise a story of differences over time, and of a culmination of these differences in a fundamental separation from the infinite. This separation becomes Absolute. The Fall becomes philosophically definitive of the I. Descartes can only talk about the idea of the infinite. We can talk of the infinite in terms of a totalization of the infinite in thought. The violence done by this totalization is a betrayal, as God was betrayed, of the infinite as it is. Augustine has use for Aristotle up to the point that he does violence to the infinite. Descartes avoids this violence by deferring the infinite from the essence of man. Thus, he is not guilty of Pride.

By separating the infinite from the essence of humanity, Descartes is free to use Aristotelian rationalism to totalize thinking into a "substance." It is, of course, Berkeley who takes Cartesian rationalism to its Anaxagorian extreme when he maintains that "there is no such thing as parts infinitely small, or an infinite number of parts contained in any finite quantity."[26]

When Berkeley turns to God we see again the closeness of the Infinite with God. He writes, "whithersoever we direct our view, we do at all times and in all places perceive manifest tokens of Divinity: everything we see, hear, feel, or anywise perceive by sense being a sign or effect of the power of God; as is our perception of those very motions which are produced by men." And so God is that very light by which Mind is illuminated and this illumination is infinite; that is beyond immediate comprehension while always being that which is comprehended—immanence. With God's immanence, Berkeley proposes to resolve the problem of the human relation to the infinite as this relation defines what it means to be human. It is precisely this relation between humanity and the infinite that, as I see it, is the crux of Cartesianism properly understood. The relation of the I is defined by its understanding of this "idea of the infinite." It is as if, for Descartes, what makes us human is this very idea, and it appears so innocuously within *Discourse on Method*, and also in the *Meditations*. This understanding of Descartes, and the philosophy that lead him to his ideas, informs Husserlian phenomenology and beyond, influencing Levinas well into the twentieth century. By adopting the Platonic interpretation of Anaxagoras' theory of soul, Descartes has cemented the aporia of the identity of mind and body, thus problematized the relation of the I to the infinite solely in terms of embodiment.

RECAPITULATION

The philosophical prejudices against which I struggle perpetuate a metaphysics of separation. This fundamental separation from the infinite is symbolized in the Adamic Myth of the Fall, which describes mankind's place in the big picture, so to speak. The biblical understanding of man as a body animated by a vital "breath" proved to have analogues in Greek philosophy, particularly in Aristotle's treatment of psuchē. However, Platonic theories focusing on the indestructibility of the Soul and its immortal existence seemed more ethically efficacious to early Christian theologians than was Aristotle's superficially un-spiritual analysis of the necessarily embodied life force. The ethical imperative of Platonism wins out in the religious philosophy of the church fathers so that when Descartes, situated at the dawn of the Modern Period and on the cusp of the Scientific Age, begins to consider the Self, he must do so as it relates to this idea of the infinite in God. And haunting this entire discussion has been the ghost of Anaxagoras, to whom everyone involved refers in their many lengthy dissertations.

We see then how the atheism that begins to emerge in the nineteenth century leads eventually to philosophies whose conclusion is that existence is Absurd. The idea of the infinite attaches the Infinite to a theistic deity so securely that the movement toward scientific explanation effectively erases the Infinite from theoretical considerations by eliminating God. Infinity is reduced to some form of indeterminacy. Such formulations of atheism are purely negative however, and as such are not so much an account of something as they are a refutation of a specific theoretical framework: that of Judeo-Christian Theistic Deism. Thus, prejudices emerging from the aporetic origin of the Self begin to determine even rejections of those very prejudices. This realization ought to serve as a sign of caution as we proceed into our Studies. Specifically, we ought take heed in our critical remarks that proper attention is paid to the consequences of our conclusions. How are we responding and to what? With these considerations in mind, I move forward.

THE CRITIQUE OF ONTOLOGY

The following two Studies are best described as a critique of ontology. At least two distinct ontological approaches are to be discussed. The Second Study will focus on the ontological primacy of presence. Figures most often associated with this line of ontological theory are Edmund Husserl and Jean-Paul Sartre. It will be shown in what ways this approach is problematic and how a redefinition of the Other can help to alleviate these problems. Specifically, the Second Study asks us to consider the role of the transcendent in philosophy and offers some insight on how the transcendent might be reintegrated in the post-modern (or post-post-modern) discussion of Selfhood.

The Third Study will discuss what I will call Negative Ontology. This is an ontology that is based almost exclusively on negation and demands the ontological primacy of exteriority. Its primary concern is with elucidating what concepts are not by reduction and linguistic equivocation. As such, the term "negative ontology" is descriptive of what that ontological method does, which is that it negates.

These two Studies, together constituting the critical movement of the current thesis, will each demand their own approaches. Each addresses very different problems within philosophies of the Self, within an account of the I. In order to facilitate this diversity, I do not wish to immediately abandon the notion of "origins." To begin the critical analysis, I will engage origins from the phenomenological perspective. In the current Study, we have conducted a largely historical analysis. In the Third Study, it will be necessary to address the phenomenology of origins so that the problems specific to an ontology of presence can be brought to light. More to the point, we must account, by accounting for the origin, for the passage of the I from non-existence into existence. I will argue that an ontology of presence cannot account for this passage and in fact this movement from non-existence into existence is the first step toward unearthing a fundamental alterity.

Notes to the Second Study

[1] Laozi, *Daodejing*, trans. Edmund Ryden, (Oxford: Oxford University Press, 2008), 5.

[2] Friedrich Nietzsche, "The Prejudices of Philosophers." *Basic Writings of Nietzsche,* trans. Walter Kaufmann, (New York: The Modern Library, 2000), 200. Important to note Nietzsche is describing here a primary philosophical prejudice, one whose valuation shades metaphysical logic. In many ways the following section extends the Nietzschean description, illustrating the philosophical legacy of the Myth of the Fall.

[3] All Biblical accounts addressed within this thesis are from *The New English Bible with Apocrypha*, (New York: Cambridge University Press, 1972). All citations referring to Biblical passages will refer to this edition of the *New English Bible*. Hereafter, references to this

text will appear as parenthetic citations in the standard Book, Chap:Verse form (i.e., Genesis, 1:1).

[4] "Introduction to the Old Testament," *New English Bible*, xv.

[5] Aristotle, "On the Soul." *The Complete Works of Aristotle Revised Oxford Translation Vol. 1 Princeton/Bollingen Series LXXI.2*, ed. Jonathan Barnes, (Princeton: Princeton University Press, 1984), 657. Hereafter, parenthetic references within the text will indicate the marginal pagination of this edition.

[6] Lloyd P. Gerson, "What is Platonism?" *Journal of the History of Philosophy* 43:3 (2005); 253—76.

[7] John M. Copper ed, "Cratylus." *Plato: Complete Works*, trans. C. D. C. Reeve, (Cambridge: Hackett Publishing, 1997), 101—56. Subsequent references to this work will be cited by parenthetical reference to the marginal pagination of this text.

[8] S. Radhakrishna, "Introduction." *The Principle Upaniṣads*, (New Delhi: HarperCollins India, 2007), 22.

[9] See, for instance, John Bussanich, "The Roots of Platonism and Vedānta: Comments on Thomas McEvilley." *International Journal of Hindu Studies* 9:1/3 (January 2005), 10.

[10] See Jeremy M. Schott, " 'Living Like a Christian, but Playing the Greek': Accounts of Apostasy and Conversion in Porphyry and Eusebius." *Journal of Late Antiquity* 1:2 (Fall 2008), 276. For more on "imagined communities," see Benedict Anderson, *Imagined Communities: Reflections on the Origin and Spread of Nationalism*, (London: Verso, 1991).

[11] "Introduction." *The New English Bible*, xv.

[12] St. Augustine, *The Confessions*, trans. Albert Cook Outler, (New York: Dover, 2002), 62.

[13] Ibid, 77.

[14] Ibid, 129.

[15] Nietzsche, "The Prejudices of Philosophers," 203.

[16] From St. Augustine, *On Genesis*, trans. Roland J. Teske, S.J. (Washington, DC: The Catholic University of America Press, 1991); 104—5.

[17] Ibid, 106.

[18] St Augustine, *Sermo* XXX-VIII, ii, 3. *Library of the Fathers of the Holy Catholic Church*, eds. E. P. Pusey, J. H. Newman, J. Keble, and C. Merriot, (Oxford; J. H. Parker, 1838—85).

[19] St. Augustine, *Eighty-Three Different Questions*, trans. David L. Mosher, (Washington DC: The Catholic University of America Press, 1982), 41.

[20] St. Augustine, *Confessions*, 62.

[21] Friedrich Nietzsche, "What is Religious?" *Basic Writings of Nietzsche,* trans. Walter Kaufmann, (New York: The Modern Library, 2000), 257.

[22] Ibid; 254—255.

[23] St. Thomas Aquinas, *Summa Theologiae*, I, q. 2 a. 3, trans. George Brantl in *Great Religions of Modern Man: Catholicism*, (New York: George Braziller, 1962), 30—32.

[24] "*I think hence I am*…I attentively examined what I was, and as I observed that I could suppose that I had no body, and that there was no world nor any place in which I might be; by that I could not therefore suppose that I was not; and that, on the contrary, from the very circumstance that I thought to doubt of the truth of other things, it most clearly and certainly followed that I was; while on the other hand, if I had only ceased to think, although all the other objects which I had ever imagined had been in reality existent, I would have had no reason to believe that I existed; I thence concluded that I was a substance whose whole essence or nature consists only in thinking, and which, that it may exist, has no need of place, nor is dependent on any material things; so that "I," that is to say the mind by which I am what I am, is wholly distinct from the body, and is even more easily known than the latter, and is such, that although the latter were not, it would still continue to be all that it is." René Descartes, "Discourse on Method." *The Rationalists*, trans. John Veitch, (New York: Anchor Books, 1974), 63.

[25] Kathleen Freeman, *Ancilla to the Pre-Socratics*, (Cambridge: Harvard University Press, 1983), 84.

[26] See Berkeley, "A Treatise Concerning the Principles of Human Knowledge." *The Empiricists*, (New York: Anchor Books, 1974), 205.

Third Study: Circumspect Origins

If you don't remember, then I remember for you: the memory of you can pass, grammatically speaking at least, for your memory, and I am perfectly willing to grant for the sake of an ornate phrase that if, after your death, I and the world still endure, it is only because you recollect the world and me.[1]

THE PROBLEM PRESENTED BY THE ANALYTICS OF ORIGIN

When embodiment is seen to be the primary aporia of the I it is inevitable that ontological speculation will turn to presence as a primary or foundational characteristic of the Self. However, the ontological I requires its own self-evidence to manifest as a presence of the Same to the Same. This is problematic in terms of self-reference, more so when we seek epistemological certainty regarding the self and the origins that situate it in the present. What happens when I seek out my own origin?

Each time I approach my own origin, I find myself not-yet-present. This not-yet-present is the non-existence, mentioned in the previous study, which precedes my existence. The miraculous coming into being is *my own* coming into being as follows from the ontological question. If I am present in posing the question of the "I," then my origin is resigned to the past from which I now demand an answer. From where did "I" come? To this the past must answer and yield my origin. Thus, my origin is not some *a priori* concept that lends me an identity, but a process of historicizing my past in order to account for how I came to be. It is at once the story of my birth and more than merely *an* event, such as the localized happening of my biological birth. Here "birth" will refer to this biological aspect in such a way that "birth" refers to an event that happened and has obtained a particular historical context in the filial lives of the people involved. Origin proper, as we shall see, outstrips or overflows this historical locality.

This overflow denies a strict analytical examination exactly because it overflows the terms upon which an analytics would operate. This will be shown, in part, by a refutation of what I term the "Sartrean Argument" and that is anything to the effect that an ontological problem can be resolved by the ontological primacy of objectivity over subjectivity. As Sartre has it:

> The for-itself is always in suspense because its being is a perpetual reprieve. If it could ever join with its being, then the otherness would by the same stroke disappear and along with it possibles, knowledge, the world. Thus the *ontological* problem of knowledge is resolved by the affirmation of the ontological primacy of the in-itself over the for-itself.[2]

Superficially, the argument is circular because it attempts to resolve the problem of ontological knowledge by making a knowledge claim in regard to ontology itself, namely the claim of the ontological primacy of the in-itself. But more to our current concerns, the conclusion is built upon the earlier claim that:

> Thus from its first arising, consciousness by the pure nihilating movement of reflection makes itself *personal*; for what confers personal existence on a being is not the possession of an Ego—which is only the *sign* of the personality—but it is the fact that the being exists for itself as a presence to itself.[3]

I shall not refute this line of thinking by affirming an inversion of the direction of primacy thereby saying that the for-itself is ontologically primary over the in-itself. First, we must be clear on how the "in-itself" and the "for-itself" are to be understood. Instead of meeting Sartre's terms, I refute his conclusions by offering a third ontological possibility in the immanence of *otherness*. What is meant by this immanence will be explicated. Before this explanation let us turn to the concepts of the for-itself and in-itself.

The problem presented by the analytics of origin is the indeterminate disruption of terms that occurs within the origin itself. Sartre was, in his own way, attempting to provide just such an analytics by the analysis of the *pour-soi* and the *en-soi*. These two terms function as a basis upon which the ontology of *Being and Nothingness* rests its formidable edifice. It is only natural that one displays the "essence" nothingness while the other hangs onto being. The for-itself personifies nothingness as negation and Sartre provides an account of the *origin* of this negation and in this account is his definition of the "I," that which is for-itself, as negation.[4] We find the repetition of "consciousness is consciousness of…" borrowed from Husserl to imply the presence of oneself to oneself. The consciousness of consciousness renders a duality that is only verbalized and never substantively actualized because there seems to be nothing which can separate the consciousness of consciousness from consciousness itself. If this separation is pursued, the unity of conscious experience is shattered and the separation immediately vanishes under the shadow of consciousness' pure immanence. The repetition of the phrase "consciousness is always consciousness of" uses the written word to imply the discrete apprehension of this presence by illustrating that the shattered unity of consciousness is immediately subsumed in the immanence of the "consciousness *of*." We write "consciousness" as a disjointed, discrete phenomenon and then immediately "consciousness of" rejoins the discrete phenomenon with the remaining phenomena of which consciousness is conscious. Thereby, we at once reveal the phenomena that are not themselves consciousness. Nothingness replaces the infinite in an inverse Cartesianism wherein the ontological primacy rests on exteriority, on being in-itself, instead of on the *cogito* and what reveals it. Much as Marx places Hegel on his head, so Sartrean ontology, in its defiance of God, places Cartesian dualism on its head in a vain hope of complicating the duality within itself into a free-ranging multiplicity of becoming.

However, as the inversion of Cartesianism, the Sartrean Argument is clearly dualistic no matter how the shattered may be reunified. Time does not take a strong enough hold in this mode of existential thought and leads us into many an impasse on the course to its conclusions. Strange that time is so lightly considered, granted the weight of history normally associated with Marx who, as Sartre himself notes, formulated what would be adopted as the core principle of existential philosophy. Sartre confesses that existentialism merely takes as its fundamental affirmation what Marx had already concluded, which was "the primacy of existence over consciousness."[5] Perhaps, if existentialism proves to maintain the parasitic relation to Marxism that Sartre claimed for it, then we will be led with it into the same nest of contradictions that Hannah Arendt noted in traditional Marxism in the essay "Tradition and the Modern Age." She writes,

> In Marx's philosophy, which did not so much turn Hegel upside down as invert the traditional hierarchy of thought and action, of contemplation and labor, and of philosophy and politics, the beginnings made by Plato and Aristotle prove their vitality by leading Marx into flagrantly contradictory statements, mostly in that part of his teaching usually called utopian.[6]

I believe Sartre's idea of radical freedom is an adequate substitution for "utopian" in Arendt's analysis. By this, I mean that a Sartrean utopia is one in which we are radically, absolutely free, and yet somehow also ethically responsible for ourselves. This is, in many ways, contradictory, at least as Sartre expresses it. In what way does my freedom oblige me? Simply to choose—and then, what does this freedom mean? And so Descartes shows his vitality by revealing the dualisms in Sartre, not only in his ontology, but also in his unwillingness to reconcile obligation to the Other and freedom. For Sartre, these terms become definitive of one another in an antithetical sort of way. Radical freedom is a freedom that foregoes all ethical restrictions while constituting the terms upon which ethics are elaborated. This duality of "free and responsible" divides our actions in the same way that mind and body divides our being.

THE CIRCUMSPECTIVE APPROACH TO THE ORIGIN

The origin is my coming into being. Through the origin I become present. What a circumspective analysis of origin will reveal is that any claimed "presence to itself" is not at all transparent. Rather, it is opaque. It is opaque because it is the presentation of another. Another speaks for me of my own origin. In doing so, the other presents me to myself after the fact. For me to speak of my own origin I must always speak through another and, therefore, I am speaking *of* another. This circumspection is carried out in order to avoid silence on the subject of origin. However, this circumspection reveals me to be something never immediately present to itself. Speaking directly of origin I speak of that which is not-yet-present. Speaking circumspectively, I speak of that which is other-to-itself. These two concepts will be made clear through the circumspective analysis of the origin. It is by the detour through these concepts that we arrive, finally, at our own opacity. At our own "otherness." The circumspective analysis of origin will show "I" to be something that is always other, thus never in its own presence.

THE SILENCE OF THE NOT-YET-PRESENT

An illumination of the concept of not-yet-present will justify the silence prescribed by direct argumentation regarding origin, particularly in the analytic mode. This preliminary consideration will lay the groundwork for our detour through the other on the approach to the origin we seek. To be clear, I use the term "origin" and its plural to refer to my own origin, generally, the origin of the "I."

I was born somewhere: from the moment I am "brought into the world" I perceive this world as a series of changes and reestablishments starting from this place which I did not choose and which I cannot find in my memory...My birth is an event for others, not for myself.[7]

The absence of my birth from memory refers us to the not-yet-present. I cannot access my birth through memory from the perspective of the here and now. The "here and now" is very often presented as something *primordial*. Let us examine this term "primordial" as it refers to consciousness and to our awareness as such. "Here and now" is primordinal in that the present is intended to designate my presence, to designate my own self-immanence. The implication of the "n" into primordi(n)al precisely where the written form differs from "prime ordinal" draws out their twofold implications. Primordinal is primordially "here"—an immanent presence—while being prime ordinally "now"—the immanent present.

As Ricoeur observes, I cannot access my birth from the here and now. My memory lapses long before the moment of my birth. The "here and now" is where I am presently. This is all that we can mean by a "primordinal" character, a character marked by a presence from which I open upon former and future presents. Primordinal implies possibility (in a sense denoting spatiality) and openness (in a sense denoting temporality) showing the inextricability of one from the other so both are implied in the utterance of one. The present is "from where" I am, the origin is not this "from where." The origin speaks of something that is not yet here coming into a former present.

At the origin I find myself not-yet-present. This results from the inaccessibility of my birth from the here and now. Once I recognize that I am "here now" my birth is committed to the past beyond me. My origin is concluded after my birth. The origin includes my birth as an opening within an enclosure. I may include many things that precede my historical birth, such as familial lineage, cultural narrative, traditional prerogatives, and ritualized behavioral roles. I may similarly include things occurring after the historical event of my birth such as language acquisition, familial functionality, role fulfillment, and behavioral expectations. These aspects bleed into the earliest memories of myself, but the lapse in experiential continuity within memory creates the element of non-reflexivity in these past developments. Any time I consider a "now" that has passed I consider it from the perspective of the present from which I reflect upon the past. *The representation of my past is really a representation, in the present, of a representation of the past.* My origin has eluded me in memory. The past that delimits has opened on the transitive present—it is *my* past, the past that is mine which opens from the birth within my origin. But I talk of *my* birth as mine though I have no memory of it. Instead I have claimed the memories of others in the identification of my birth. So I have uncovered my birth and part of this uncovering was a recovering from others.

My origin is concealed from the outset because it is terminated by my presence and so is a history I am not present to experience. The origin comes to me only when another presents it to me. When I understand that my origin is the presentation of another I realize that origins are concealed. On the detour through the other I do the work of "unconcealing" my origin. The truth of origins is the truth of another, as the meaning of "truth" stems from the Greek ἀλήθεια. Consider here Heidegger's translation of ἀλήθεια as "unconcealedness."[8] He claims that ἀλήθεια still resonates in the modern notion of "subjectivity of the spirit," and, when we properly understand this concept, that it has nothing to do with "subjectivism."[9] The "subjectivity of the spirit" is what is present in the now and that we always associate with a particular embodiment of subjectivity, consciousness, or being over time. In the current inquiry this subjectivity is said to be "mine." With ἀλήθεια as unconcealedness the truth of any matter is something toward which one must struggle. If I take my origin without this struggle I have not done the work necessary to uncovering myself. The ownership of myself comes to me from another, and so without the detour through the other I cannot reach the origin in order to speak of it. Mention of origin betrays this detour from the outset. "Subjectivism" is avoided because it is not merely our subjectivity that denotes "I" as a sign. The subjectivity of the other is to be taken as an opacity that reflects us when we come up against it and from this encounter we claim our birth.

Lacan's concept of the mirror stage is important here. He says, "We have only to understand the mirror stage *as an identification*, in the full sense that analysis gives to the term: namely, the transformation that takes place in the subject when he assumes an image—whose predestination to this phase-effect is sufficiently indicated by the use, in analytic theory, of the ancient term *imago*."[10] While I am not practicing "analysis" as the reference here is to psycho-analysis, I am suggesting something analogous to this idea of identification as phase-effect; that is generally the culmination of a temporal process. I, like Lacan, am rejecting what he called the "Ideal-I" in favor of, as Lacan describes:

> …that this form [the I] situates the agency of the ego before its social determination, in a fictional direction, which will always remain irreducible for the individual alone, or rather, which will only rejoin the coming-into-being (*le devenir*) of the subject asymptotically, whatever the success of the dialectical syntheses by which he must resolve as *I* his discordance with his own reality.[11]

I would caution, however, not do draw reductionist conclusions from psychoanalytic talk of synthesis, for we will see that the I is not reconciled to the Other as to the Same. Thus the ego in Lacanian terminology cannot be some "Ideal-I," which Lacan has rejected. The Third Study will deal more fully with reductionist philosophy.

My subjectivity is negated through the detour. "I am not" because I attempt to claim for myself an event that is not an event for me. But the event, though preceding my presence, is intended as the event by which I become present. This is the "yet-present" of the not-yet-present. I am not negated absolutely, but my presence is provisional pending my origin. There I fall silent and another speaks for me. The not-yet-present is the cusp of origin in which I am given to presence. This presence comes, like my birth, through the other.

THE TEMPORALIZATION OF COMING INTO BEING

The explanation of the not-yet-present has shown two things. It has shown that the detour through the other is necessary to claim my origin as my own. It has also shown that origin is something specifically temporal that encompasses the birth from which I open onto the world. The not-yet implies a future now in which what is not present becomes present. The yet-present denotes the possibility of being that is to come and also implies the ghost of a presence in the anticipation of the *moment* of origin; the realization of coming into being, of my consciousness of this being. The tension can be emphasized by an expansion of the former concept of the not-yet-present. It can be expressed as the not-present-yet-present. Here, we emphasize both the negation experienced by the detour through the other and also, following this negation, our affirmation. "I am not present, yet, present." So we thus negate ourselves prior to the affirmation of ourselves. Negation is only a path to self-recognition. It leads us to the Other by denying access to ourselves in the present. We move to the detour as our origin moves us toward being here now.

A process is taking shape. The process is one of claiming a preceding event as "mine." The claim is made on my origin and that which is claimed is other.

Temporalization is implied throughout this process. There is an inescapable sense of time inhering in the concept of origins. We have touched on this above. I am now. This now stands in reference to former nows and the origin encloses our openness to the series of nows that have brought me to the present. The not-yet-present has shown this opening up to be the transit from non-being to being, from not-yet to yet-present. Likewise, I consider the specific historical event of my birth though I cannot recall that event to my memory. The event of my birth is a story that was told to me. I come into being after my birth. The origin encompasses birth. A circumspective analysis of my origin reveals it as the event by which I become present without yet being present to myself. It is the $\dot{\alpha}\lambda\dot{\eta}\theta\varepsilon\iota\alpha$ of my being and I am unconcealed by another.

SPEAKING AS THE OTHER-TO-ITSELF

I have come to the not-yet-present to claim my origin. In claiming, I find my claim is staked on another. Not merely *through* another, but *of* another. When I claim my origin, I am claiming the origin of another, and in doing so, am other-to-itself.

The other-to-itself at no time implies a duality that is actualized in a sense denoting substance. Hegel is not offended to find this difference at the very outset of identity, that we find an identity in what escapes being identical with. But neither do we find a neat synthesis of the two. The opposition stands as a result of the perpetual temporalization invoked by the reference to my origin. How then, without admitting synthesis, has Hegelian criticism been avoided? I have drawn into temporality a key movement in Hegelian logic that implies an active difference precisely at the origin and also a temporalization that occurs by the detour suggested from the start.[12] I must *move* through the other to arrive at this origin wherein I find this inherent difference. However, at no time do I synthesize the two concepts with one another. "I am" and I seek this origin that eludes me. The other offers this origin to me, they recount to me the moment of my birth, tell me the history of my family, and teach my language and custom. The recollection of my birth by another is, for the one recollecting the event, the birth of another. A fissure arises within the detour that marks me always as other-than. I am other than the one who recalls my birth. In the recollection of my birth, I am other to the one who recalls the event. And so I am presented to myself *as* another and *through* another.

The temporalization is complete at this dyadic distance from myself. I have begun (I am), through this temporal process of "othering," a presence that is never immanently present. This is the "other-to." I am always other. The moment I begin to refer to myself I become other-to, and in self-reference, reveal the "to-itself." At the instant of my self-recognition I refer myself to another and through another so that I never arrive at myself with any finality. I am never in my own presence. On this point, we have outstripped the origin we sought. Let us return to this subject.

PRESENCE AND THE ORIGIN: PART ONE

What has the origin revealed to us? It has revealed distance and also difference. It has implemented a temporal spacing that suggests a primordinal rift between the present "now" in which experience happens, including the phenomenon of consciousness, and any expression of those experiences as my experiences; as attributes of the "I" referent.

A refutation would claim that this linguistic difference does nothing to negate the *fact* of our immediate experiences, that we experience them as presence to ourselves in a way that is *more primordinal than the difference at our origin*. For the time being it is not necessary to negate the immediacy of experience. What we require is to understand these experiences, particularly the "experience" of my origin, of my beginning. I feel an intuitive desire to know my origins. Then, I must ask, how can I achieve such an understanding?

Understanding can only be achieved, on a meaningful level, by the communicability of what is to be understood. The un-interpreted sensations of my experiences do nothing to render themselves understandable. It is I who must begin the process of deciphering meaning from the "raw" experiences of everyday life. Like these "raw" experiences, I should not expect that my fledging attempts to understand be immediately discernable to me, nor should they be communicable from the very outset. Communication demands some form of language. Even given something like a brute experience, to make sense of this brute experience I must communicate the experience. Were such experiences immediately present I would have no need for the communication. But the process opening from within the origin invokes communicability in order to make sense and meaning. As soon as I begin the communication of meaning to myself I have created an other out of myself in order to transmit, from one aspect of my being to another (specifically, from myself at t_1 to myself at t_2), a meaning that I derive from a pre-experiential cognition. That is to say, an event happens, and then I experience it. As such, we can say an event happens to me and then I experience it as another.[13]

Again, I am not dually present. Temporalization disseminates the contradictions of duality in identity. But I am not immanently present either. I am always mediated, and I am mediated through another. And so, the circumspection of my origin has in fact brought me to an understanding of myself. Though I do not stand before myself (that would be a contradiction) I am, nonetheless, rendered sensible to myself, sensible and meaningful only as another. This arrival is the arrival of $\dot{\alpha}\lambda\acute{\eta}\theta\varepsilon\iota\alpha$, of my own "unconcealedness." In a sense, in the circumspective analysis, I have "found myself." But I have not found the presence *to* myself *of* myself. I have only found a way to make myself *meaningful* to myself. Notice always in my language is this fissure, this implied duality that does not admit to substance. Have we, on this point, breeched into the metaphysical?

THE TRANSCENDENT OF THE ANALYSIS

If the metaphysical has been breeched, we open ourselves to the transcendent formulation of our analysis. In the not-yet-present we have a formulation of ourselves as a negation. On the detour through the other we sought out a process, a trajectory, a movement, by which what is not-yet-present becomes present. But this presence that follows from the origin is a presence that is not present to itself. Rather, it is other-to-itself. And so the affirmative we had sought through the detour is the affirmation of the other. In essence, the metaphysical as revealed by fissure is the space between the other and myself; it is the space that the circumspective analysis attempts to traverse. I never complete this attempt; I am always in transit. There is no end to and no return from the circumspective analysis, and this is the virtue of the truth it reveals. To reach myself I go beyond myself to the other, but there is no return from the other; I end up at an origin that is another's to the other. Thus the infinite distance arises to enclose us in a *perpetual detour through the other to reach ourselves*. The strength of ἀλήθεια in the above analysis is that the struggle against our isolation in the present has driven us on a detour that leaves us stranded in the presence of another. What ἀλήθεια makes unconcealed is the immanence of the other. In the immanence of this other I find transcendence; that I transcend myself

Can I then grant the possibility of a "raw experience" as referring to a pre-theoretical phenomenon that is not capable of understanding or communication? We had formerly granted this possibility and now we must retract that admission. Here, we deepen the critique to solidify experiences as eternally understandable, communicable, and for which the terms carrying the meanings of "brute" or "raw" can only affect negation. This negation is the negation of the metaphysical, a negation that speaks only of what the transcendent is not, or that it cannot be. The affirmation of the self is at once the affirmation of the transcendent, thus is a negation of the negation of the transcendent, the ἀλήθεια of the transcendent. Already present in ἀλήθεια is the aforementioned double negative. ἀλήθεια is itself negative, it conceals a presence, negates its being, hides it, keeps it from being present. For ἀλήθεια the "α" acts just as the transliterated prefix "a" acts in "amoral," "apolitical," atheistic," or "atypical." The "a" as well as the "α" negates what follows it. And so, *ἀλήθεια* negates a negation.

Anything equivocal to "brute" or "raw" experience is thus negated by the detour through the other; it must be negated by any acknowledgement of myself. Thus, all experiences, given that they are *my* experiences are the negation of "brute" or "raw" experiences. We are always beyond ourselves when we ask from whence we came. The circumspective analysis of origins shows this transcendence and the transcendent. My origin is the transcendent of the analysis and that is why it required circumspection. It is independent of myself because it is another's. It is independent of myself because it encloses, includes that which is not yet present and anticipants this presence in its absence. Within this enclosure is an opening, the opening is an event, and this event that is not an event for me terminates in my presence and constitutes the transitional moment of my origin. In speaking of the transcendent, we have invoked the troubled spirit of philosophy: the metaphysical.

Metaphysics is a constantly recurring mode of understanding; one that is seldom utilized sensibly and often used in straw-man arguments against those who make strong claims that are difficult for others to understand. Am I speaking of that which lies "beyond the physical"? No, clearly I am not. My concern lies with my own being. If that being obtains aspects that are not physical aspects then that will require some further elucidation. Nor am I commenting on the works of Aristotle written "after the physics." I do not speak of God, or of the immortality of the soul, or of the freedom of my will. I have not even spoken directly of my origin, for it has been shown the silence recommended by such an approach. Of what have I spoken?

I have spoken of another that is myself.

RECAPITULATION

Through a refutation of the Sartrean Argument, we have shown the troubles specific to a direct analytic approach to the questions of origin, and thus, to the gateway of the ontological I. The flaw in this line of argumentation is maintained in claims on both sides of ontological primacy, of interiority in Descartes, and of exteriority in Sartre. Neither is a philosophically tenable position. If any ontological primacy is to be maintained, though I find ontological primacy a highly dubious claim in all its forms, it is maintained specifically as otherness. This troublesome issue will be addressed in the following study. In response to the polarization of Cartesian dualism and Sartrean existentialism, we have attempted a thorough temporalization of the origin in order to disrupt the totalized notions of origin found in those respective theoretical frameworks. In doing so, we have aligned ourselves closely with the thesis put forth by Emmanuel Levinas in *Totality and Infinity* and *Otherwise Than Being*. For now, we must focus on the aporia arising from the circumspective analysis, which has placed the problem of embodiment in terms of non-existence versus existence, or, to use the terms of the current work, between the not-yet-present and the other-to-itself. The not-yet-present denotes a being that is a possibility whose actualization is affirmed as though fatalistically. Temporalization takes root and pushes possibility to a terminus wherein it is consummated and brought forth within the origin. The other-to-itself is the result of this process, but the otherness denoted by this presence is an otherness internal to itself, an internalized exteriority that demands a presence it finds lacking in itself. And so, this being, whose presence is *predicted* by the not-yet-present, even *promised* within the not-yet-present, finds itself *never* present to itself and yet *perpetually* presented by another thus becoming other-to-itself. The promise of being is an impossibility that causes the promise to default into otherness. My presence is promised, and yet I am presented another. We have seen that the perspective gained through the above argumentation is not our own perspective, which we have pursued far from the encounter on the precipice. Let us return there now in order to regain that vantage so crucial to understanding the pending aporia of the ontological "I."

PRESENCE AND THE ORIGIN: PART TWO

The encounter on the precipice does not offer us a horizon that is the limitation of our being. It is precisely the unboundedness of the expanse opened by the horizon that inspires the current inquiry. There is implicit possibility and the idea of the infinite manifests in seeing "as far as the eye can see." It is this presence there on the edge that enables these relations to obtain. We must therefore be careful not to constrict the horizon with negativity without acknowledging the positivity that is the cause of my questioning.

The presence is in itself the problematic. We had made the connection to "Being-there" early in the work and it is this "being there on the precipice" that has unveiled the problematic of presence. This presence, as denoted by the "I," sees itself as this presence that is problematic, not in general, but problematic for-

and in-itself. The problematic is self-contingent. Thus we have not succumbed to placing the essence prior to existence, and thereby offended the existentialists, but neither have we insisted upon the existence preceding its essence. If anything, the circumspective origin has shown that the aporia of the ontological "I" confuses this distinction so that the essence and the existence manifest in an inter-contingent modality stemming from an openness within an enclosure. This enclosed openness at once obtains a dual ontological primacy wherein the immediate presence of consciousness is always already mediated through otherness in order to arrive at the presence it claims as identical. If the presence is the presentation of another, then the one receives this presentation as if receiving a gift, and this gift, mediated as it is, becomes a gift given by oneself to oneself. Thus being self-contingent denotes a necessary alterity.

These considerations will form the starting point of the following study. At the consideration of a negative ontology, which is descriptive of an ontological methodology of negation, we take up consideration of what the Western philosophic tradition has, since Locke, termed "the problem of personal identity." Viewed from this perspective, that of identity, of sameness, of *idem*, and the *cogito*, the gift of the presence to itself becomes an utter paradox. The gift of presence becomes an impossible gift and thus a political or economical gift that must constantly be mediated. It is this mediation that negative ontology attempts to account for by the Same as opposed to the Other. A critique of negative ontology will lead eventually to an affirmation of something beyond the Same, something specifically Other.

Notes to the Third Study

[1] Vladimir Nabokov, "Ultima Thule." *The Stories of Vladimir Nabokov*, (New York: Vintage International, 1997), 500.

[2] Jean-Paul Sartre, *Being and Nothingness*, trans. Hazel Barnes, (New York: Washington Square Press, 1992), 787.

[3] Ibid, 156—7.

[4] Ibid, 33—85.

[5] See *Search for a Method*, trans. Hazel E. Barnes, (New York: Vintage Books, 1968); 31—4.

[6] Hannah Arendt, "Tradition and the Modern Age." *Between Past and Future*, (New York, Penguin Books, 1977); 17—40.

[7] Paul Ricoeur, *Fallible Man*, (New York: Fordham University Press, 1986), 23.

[8] Martin Heidegger, *Parmenides*, (Bloomington: Indiana University Press, 1998).

[9] Ibid, 19.

[10] Jacques Lacan, "The mirror stage." *Identity: a reader*, eds. Paul du Gay, Jessica Evans, & Peter Redman, (London: SAGE Publications, 2000), 45.

[11] Ibid, 47.

[12] An important parallel here with Deconstructionism. See Jacques Derrida, *"Différance."* *Margins of Philosophy*, (Chicago: Chicago University Press, 1984), 14. The comments relate to an analysis of Hegel's *Logic* by Alexandre Koyré, "Hegel á Iena." *Etudes d'historie de la pensée philosophique*, (Paris: Armand Colin, 1961), 153—54.

[13] Derrida does much to argue for the dissolution of the dichotomy between meaning and sign that makes sense of this passage. Two essays are most notable for this work: Derrida, "Form and Meaning: A Note on the Phenomenology of Language." *Margins of Philosophy*, trans. Alan Bass, (Chicago: University of Chicago Press, 1972); 155—73. Also, Derrida, "Structure, Sign and Play in the Discourse of the Human

Sciences." *Writing and Difference*, trans Alan Bass, (Chicago: University of Chicago Press, 1978); 278—93.

Fourth Study: Negative Ontology

Not betrayed by the black blood and not willfully betrayed by his mother, but betrayed by her all the same, who had bequeathed him not only the blood of slaves but even a little of the very blood which had enslaved; himself his own battleground, the scene of his own vanquishment and the mausoleum of his defeat.[1]

SPEAKING OF WHAT IS NOT

The current study will be initiated on the grounds established by the preceding circumspective analysis of origins. Before we embark on the way to our conclusions, I will briefly recount where we've already tread so as to make the way forward more clear. From the First Study the methodological concerns of the thesis were made evident and emphasis was placed on the movement that takes place in the revelation of the I. The question was ultimately formulated: How am I mediated to myself? This question referred us to the history of philosophy which speculates on the origins of the Soul, or Self, or I. Part of knowing who I am is knowing where I came from and the historical analysis provided by the Second

Study elucidated the key elements that the ontological I will demand of any answer provided for it. For instance, the relation of the I to the infinite, the role or purpose of its life. Also, the relation of the I to its history, both conceptual and actual, and these considerations drove us to consider origins in the Third Study. The Second Study, by addressing the philosophical components of the conceptual I, had been a direct attempt to analyze the I, or at least what we've been led to assume is the I. In the Third Study, the circumspective approach led us to a different way of understanding the Self in light of differences that obtain from the Self's very origin. Such an understanding had been recommended to us by the conclusions of the Second Study, and the Third merely compiles philosophical evidence for accepting the recommendation. This brings us to the Fourth and current study, which will put this aporia into motion. The motion will commence here, but must be concluded in the following study.

In many ways, the preceding studies have spoken of what I am not. Philosophy in the mid to late twentieth century, especially in the English-speaking world, is dominated by what I will describe as a negative ontology. My predecessors oblige me to begin from a place of ontological negation. Once I begin, I will myself undertake a negation and that is of the negation of an assumed ontology—one that has been taken for granted. My "No!" implies with it a "Yes!" addressed to an entity beyond the theoretical objects of my polemic. I will be showing in what ways contemporary philosophy has spoken of what is not by outlining that which I will later affirm. This will be the project of the current Study and will lead us into the final two Studies of the current work.

THE TURN TO LANGUAGE AND REDUCTION

John Locke can be credited or blamed for initiating the discussion of "personal identity" in the English-speaking world. He was, in many ways, taking the Aristotelian insistence on the unity of mind and body against Cartesian dualism. What concerns us in the current Study is the legacy of criteria that was Locke's most evident influence on twentieth century philosophy. When Locke discusses the concept of personal identity in *An Essay Concerning Human Understanding* he does so in the manner of establishing a criterion for personal identity, particularly personal identity over time, which he considered to be problematic. Locke believes that a conception of a person as spirit alone does not constitute a person, but that a person is the combination of this mind/body. After making this premise, he moves to establish what the word "person" stands for, which he believes to be: "a thinking intelligent being, that has reason and reflection, and can consider itself as itself, the same thinking thing, in different times and places;" but he goes on to ask further: "whether it be the same identical substance?"[2] It is established that consciousness is the cause of identity over time, as consciousness unites present and past action via memory, and that substance is essentially irrelevant to selfhood. This line of argumentation is developed into the Psychological Criterion for personal identity over time. Locke writes, "Nothing but consciousness can unite remote existences into the same person; the identity of substance will not do it. For whatever substance there is, however framed, without consciousness there is no person…"[3] Locke's treatment expresses the Aristotelian matter-of-factness regarding selfhood that we had addressed in the Second Study. Locke's treatment of personal identity is brief, relative to the overall length of the *Essay*, yet it had a profound effect on the course of philosophy. This effect must be briefly outlined.

First, we can see that Locke's theory is much more coherent within the scientific worldview, which was becoming increasingly influential when Locke was alive, between 1632 and 1704. His emphasis on memory will only become more relevant with the emergence of psychology as a scientific field and as consciousness takes on central roles in the philosophies of Kant and Hegel. Criticism of Locke as a memory theorist largely misses the point of the activity of consciousness bringing divergent materials into identity with one another. Consciousness, following Locke's text, cannot be equivocated to memory. Thus, philosophers have often focused on the conceptual analysis and metaphysics of Locke's theory without giving thought to the *psychology* of identity via memory.[4] It is rather the question of "what constitutes personhood over time?" that predominates English-speaking philosophers in the twentieth century.

We begin with Bernard Williams, who wants to illustrate two principle limitations on how thought experiments are to be constructed for philosophical analysis and on how to interpret these various constructions. The specific thought experiment Williams wants us to consider is the following: "Suppose that there were some process to which two persons, *A* and *B*, could be subjected as a result of which they might be said—question beggingly—to have *exchanged bodies*."[5] Why would he be concerned with clarifying the use of such an experiment? It seems to me that it is precisely the thought experiment explained by Williams that Locke himself used to establish consciousness as the criterion for personal identity. Locke writes:

> Whether, if the same thinking substance (supposing immaterial substances only to think) be changed, it can be the same person? I answer, That cannot be resolved except by those who know what kind of substances they are that do think, and whether the consciousness of past actions can be transferred from one thinking substance to another.[6]

Locke has us consider the case of a prince and a cobbler who we imagine to have switched bodies while retaining the consciousness associated with their original bodies. Under Locke's theory, the prince in the cobbler's body is still the same person as when the prince had his own body and the cobbler is still the cobbler even when his consciousness is transplanted into the prince's body.[7] Similar examples recur throughout the discourse on this subject.

Williams is expanding upon this initial thought and setting conditions by which we may establish how it is that the two persons are or are not identical; that is, whether or not this transfer of consciousness really occurred. Considerations such as these are not foreign to philosophy; recall Descartes' invocation of the Great Deceiver. But Williams, now with an entirely different agenda than Descartes, wants the thought experiment to perform very specific functions within an analytics of personal identity. There is a specifically linguistic turn to analytic philosophy that is much different from the religious turn of Augustine and Descartes. This linguistic turn results from the demand for the rigor of science in philosophy.

Robert Nozick attempts to elucidate Williams' point more clearly and formulates a theory of personal identity he calls the "Closest Continuer Theory." The Closest Continuer Theory presents the necessary condition for identity as being: "something at t_2 is not the same entity as x at t_1 if it is not x's closest continuer. And 'closest' means closer than all others; if two things at t_2 tie in closeness to x at t_1, then neither is the same entity as x."[8] This theory is going to provide us with the re-emergence of our old aporia, which, if we remember from the First Study, was primarily an issue of embodiment. Now the criterion moves to what will constitute this "closest continuer." Naturally, the two immediate contenders are best described as the physical criterion and the psychological criterion. I see a pattern here, but let us follow this line of thinking about criteria for a bit longer, if only to produce a heightened clarity of the aporetic structure of the I.

Why do I claim that this brand of philosophizing is specifically linguistic? By and large, what this type of identity theory does is reduce personhood to a totalized referent for which the sign is "I." Now, the question, from the linguistic perspective, is this: Does the sign "I" refer to the selfsame substance at t_1 as it does at t_2. The I is merely a linguistic referential that must be determined by some criterion. Derek Parfit, like Hume, takes this logic to its most extreme formulation and, in doing so, believes himself to have proven the irrelevance of personal identity to survival.[9] Hume, of course, believes the *cogito* to be a mythical entity whose existence was such that:

> ...all the nice and subtle questions concerning personal identity can never possibly be decided, and are to be regarded rather as grammatical than as philosophical difficulties. Identity depends on the relations of ideas; and these relations produce identity, by means of that easy transition they occasion. But as the relations, and the easiness of the transition may diminish by sensible degrees, we have no just standard, which we can decide any dispute concerning the time, when they acquire or lose a title to the name of identity.[10]

Like Hume's skeptical empiricism dissolved the unifying effects of Lockean consciousness, Parfit's reductionism dissolves the entity to which the "I" refers into a series of relations that hold more or less precisely the relation of identity. The relation of identity is labeled "Relation R," which is: "psychological connectedness over and/or psychological continuity, with the right kind of cause."[11] Parfit is attempting to incorporate Nozick's admission of degrees of identity in regards to personhood while at the same time reducing personhood to a conceptual relation that is referenced by language. Like all Reductionist theories of the twentieth century, Parfit's ultimate goal is an impersonal articulation of personhood, thus, the achievement of a scientifically, read logically rigorous, formula for personhood that can be either identical or not identical in terms of *sameness*. It is on this point that the analytic philosophy of personal identity will fail, just as Sartre's analytics was shown to fail in the Second Study. It is

I AM NOT THE SIGN I SIGNAL MYSELF BY

Consider these words, those of Emmanuel Levinas: "He who signals himself by a sign qua signifying that sign is not the signified of the sign—but delivers the sign and gives it."[12] What does this statement mean in the context of our current thesis? For one, it will point us to an insight formulated by Hegel; and here, when we consider Hegel, we must be careful to note Levinas' critique of Hegelian philosophy as fulfilling an "Odyssey" of the Spirit back to its home in Truth. We ought take heed to break, with Levinas, from Hegel's circular pattern and consider the "rectilinear" pattern of Abraham on a voyage, into ethics, without return.[13] Secondly, it reveals the annihilating function of negative ontology that will, in fact, *undermine its logical rigor by excluding certain necessary variables from consideration.* This will make more sense of the connection made between St. Augustine and Nietzsche in the Study most exclusively directed toward the history of philosophy.

I am not the sign I signal myself by. If we accept this claim then, reductionist arguments such as Parfit's, and those of identity over time forwarded by Williams and Nozick, collapse. All of these arguments treat personal identity in terms of sameness. But this is clearly not the concern for survival, nor was it the concern of Locke in his analysis. And in fact Locke had made this quite clear when he writes,

> Could we suppose any spirit wholly stripped of all its memory or consciousness of past actions, as we find our minds are of a great part of ours...the union or

> separation of such a spiritual substance would make no variation of personal identity any more than that of any particle of matter does... Any substance vitally united to the present thinking being, is a part of that very same self which now is: anything united to it by a consciousness of former actions, makes also a part of the same self, which is the same both then and now,[14]

We ought see that he is emphasizing the *connectedness* of differing substances (which are not identical) over time by an active consciousness that *makes those divergent substances selfsame by an act of will, rendering them coherent in a Self*. But Locke takes us beyond identity theory to *ethics* when he describes the refent "persons" to denote "a forensic term appropriating actions and their merit; and so belongs only to intelligent agents capable of a law, and happiness and misery."[15] I employ a Kantian interpretation of Locke's theory, thus disarming the Humean effects of reductionism on theories of Selfhood, and showing the problem of "personal identity" to be merely linguistic paradox. Kant sees consciousness as active, assembling its experiences from sense data by virtue of certain functions of the mind outlined in the Twelve Categories. Space and Time are, of course, a medium through which consciousness is open to having experiences; experience happens *in* space and time, so to speak.[16] From this perspective, Locke's consciousness is performing the function of bringing actually non-identical substances into formal identity through the unifying activity of memory. I can then endorse Christine Korsgaard's refutation of the Reductionist theory of personal identity; the most important aspect of which involves Parfit's inability to differentiate between the theoretical, or formal, and the practical standpoint. Parfit's reduction is a linguistic formalism that does nothing to negate the actual phenomenon of identity as people experience it.[17] The only problem with the Kantian approach enters when it asks us to incorporate some transcendental ego, which is itself but a sign for the I (as is "the I"), and I have adopted the phenomenological method in the hopes of avoiding just this problem. On the distinction between the empirical and transcendental self, Kant writes:

> The 'I think' expresses the act of determining my existence. Existence is already given thereby, but the mode in which I am to determine this existence, that is, the manifold belonging to it, is not thereby given. In order that it be given, self-intuition is required; and such intuition is conditioned by a given *a priori* form, namely, time, which is sensible and belongs to the receptivity of the determinable [in me]. Now since I do not have another self-intuition which gives the *determining* in me (I am conscious only of the spontaneity of it) prior to the act of *determination* [*vor dem Aktus des Bestimmens*], as time does in the case of the determinable, I cannot determine my existence as that of a self-active being; all that I can do is to represent to myself the spontaneity of my thought, that is, of the determination; and my existence is still only determinable sensibly, that is as the existence of

an appearance. But is owing to this spontaneity that I
entitle myself *intelligence*.[18]

Here, Kant admits the self as only manifest (given) to us as an appearance, whereas I want to disrupt the "givenness" of this appearance by the ethical call emanating from the Other. This call signals beyond the appearance of the I. And so, the transcendental ego resolves to be more formal than will do for our current project and must be categorized along with the other formalities that suggest the Same. I include this lengthy passage from *Critique of Pure Reason* in order that we may contrast it with that of Hegel's, which follows:

> ...the self is a *Subject* to which the content is related as Accident and Predicate. This Subject constitutes the basis to which the content is attached, and upon which the movement runs back and forth. Speculative thinking behaves in a different way. Since the Notion is the object's own self, which presents itself as the *coming-to-be of the object*, it is not a passive Subject inertly supporting the Accidents; it is, on the contrary, the self-moving Notion which takes its determinations back into itself. In this movement the passive subject perishes; it enters into differences and the content, and constitutes the determinateness, i.e. the differentiated content and its movement, instead of remaining over and against it.[19]

We compare this to Kant and from a synthesis of the two are able to derive a self-active being, something that Kant did not intuit via the transcendental aesthetic. We must be careful, however, not to follow Hegel too far from Kant, to the point where we admit a totalized, reconciled being who is the "Same as itself," so to speak. This passage from Hegel merely makes relevant the work done by the Third Study to a critical revision of a basically Kantian position on the self. Therefore, the I is not some entity over and above the experiential consciousness aware of itself reflectively. The I only comes about through its interaction with the world and, through this interaction, is revealed to itself as itself. This *coming-to-be of the object* was really the focus of the Third Study. But what this means for us now is that a philosophically acute understanding of personal identity demands us to see beyond the sign of the I. In order to engage in discussions of the self, I have utilized a wide lexical categorization of the I. Soul, self, subject, I: these are but the signs by which I indicate a particular phenomenon, a phenomenon upon which I focus while on the precipice. In fact, the totalization of myself into these signs is the first way in which violence is done to me. This violence is the initiation of objectification. I shall return to this theme as a concern of ethics. Ethics need not necessarily condemn this violence in itself, for this rupture, or fissure is the location of our grasp on the world and the lever on the crux of our understanding. Ethics must later concern itself only with the possibility of the use of this basic violence as the actual annihilation of the Other.

For a moment, I will elucidate the relevance of the previous Study. In the beginning I come into self-awareness through the signs, given by others, that indicate me to myself. I come to see myself as an "I" by connecting, through the mnemonic functions of consciousness, the various ways in which the other presents me to myself. I am a part of a family, a speaker of a language, gendered, a student, a child, adolescent, a member of a particular social class; all of these forms of identification are assimilated in one way or another, or rather, they are disseminated and dissimulated among us. I come to recognize myself as something more than the signs I give to indicate myself. The dissimulation of my identity behind the sign is only the product of a dissemination of the excess of the thematizing function of the sign. What I mean is this; my father indicates me with a sign that thematizes me into an image of his own construction: the amalgamation of myself with, for instance, the ideal of the star athlete. I have thus become an object that is deployed, as a soldier is deployed, into the historical scheme of a project in which I have a specifically assigned role; for instance, to win the ball game. I am determined to have some objective qua this objectification. This is, of course, what philosophers have done on the theoretical plane. My self is thematized to be some ideal of the transcendental ego, or the immortal soul, or the *cogito*, etc. This sign, this subject as object, the formal, theoretical equivalent of myself, is at once more than I can ever be while never being what I wholly am. It robs me of my potential, of my ability to surprise, by casting me in the totality. Because thematization comes from the other, it surpasses my ability to meet with the imagination of that other. Indeed, I am left guessing as to what expectations this imagination has set for me, and so in any attempt to meet the expectations of the other, I form an economy with the other to whom I now present myself in turn.

The process, now reciprocating, becomes the processes by which I am continually coming to know myself. Again, we come upon that pervasive feeling in which the I that I am coming to know is other to me, and so that I am other to myself. Let us turn now to objectification as problematic.

REBELLION AND OBJECTIFICATION

A useful descriptive term for the process by which one person forms a totalizing description of another person is objectification. There is a plenitude of ways in which we are objectified which may be pragmatic rather than problematic. But I want to suggest that objectification carries the possibility of a specific problematic; it is the problem of any negative ontology. In normal, we might say healthy, circumstances people can remain open to one another, and thus permit the boundaries of the signs being used for indication to be permeable. For instance, gender roles may not be rigorously defined by exclusive terms that separate men and women in their activities and responsibilities. In these instances, I do not define signs of reference as being objectifying; indeed, they are often affirming in these contexts. Remember, totalization here is an indication of violence, and so objectification too implies violence done to a person. The violence of objectification is the annihilation of my potentiality for being under the totalizing function of an imposed signifier. Of course, this is actualized in instances of slavery, forced labor, domestic violence, rape, child abuse, and any form of bigotry. Obviously, such a list is far from complete, the unfortunate consequence of the human imagination given over to wantonness and irrationality in violence.

Luce Irigaray comments:

> Others were only copies of the idea of man, a potentially perfect idea, which all the more or less imperfect copies had to struggle to equal. These copies were, moreover, not defined in and of themselves, in other words, as a different subjectivity, but rather, were defined in terms of an ideal subjectivity and as a function of their inadequacies with respect to that ideal: age, reason, race, culture, and so on.[20]

These words introduce a critique of Simone de Beauvoir that can be described as an inversion of the feminist rejection of Otherness. In refusing to be the Other, femininity has reduced itself to the Same, leaving historical masculine hegemony intact. For Irigaray, the question of the other is poorly formulated in terms of the "other of the same." We should rather see the other as an/other subject [*un autre sujet*][21] that is irreducible and deserving of equal dignity. When I understand objectification as violence, I am moved with Irigaray to emphasize a reformulation of Other in terms that destabilized and decentralized Same. This destabilization is the project, as I see it, of Paul Ricoeur in *Oneself as Another*. In this text, the focus is on the disruption of *idem* identity by narrativity in favor of a differentiating *ipseity* that denoted a character peculiar to each subject, thereby each subject may become another.[22]

However, we must take into account the actual objectification of this differentiated subject. Consider the following expression of an objectified subject: "I walked down Capitol Street feeling that the sidewalk was unreal, that I was unreal, that the people were unreal, yet expecting somebody to demand to know what right I had to be on the streets."[23] An absurd situation; unreal, demoralized, yet expected to justify this unreal existence to a demand from another who *is* real and whose demand for rights conceals a threat of violence should those rights be found lacking. Richard Wright, being the black man who authored the words above, did not possess the requisite rights; he would not have been able to justify himself to an authority, thus his dilemma. He is objectified in the following way: As a black man in the South, Wright must address white people as "sir," "madam," "mister," and so on. A white man, Pease, receives a report from a white co-worker named Reynolds that Wright fails to address Pease as "Mr." Now, Wright is objectified as "The Black Man." He is *wrong no matter what*. Regardless of whether or not Wright addresses Pease with a "Mister," Wright is going to come out the "nigger." If Wright says he *does in fact* call Pease "Mr. Pease," then he is by inference calling Reynolds a liar. However, if Wright admits he never addresses Mr. Pease as such, he admits to being a black man insulting a white man in the South. Wright's potential has been totalized and in this instance that totalization has led to a completely negative outcome for Wright; an outcome determined by reference to Wright's "blackness." Irigaray would point out that the ideal Subject is by default "white" and so, in the misguided terminology of traditional philosophies of the Same, Richard must be the default, and defective, Other. In order to claim his Otherness as a component of his radical individuation, Richard will have to rebel against his objectification.

Before moving on, I would like to discuss a less obvious way in which objectification enters into unethical behaviors, one that will perhaps address the routine lives of those not living a marginalized existence within their societies. Consider Lady Bathsheba and her maidservant Liddy in the novel *Far from the Madding Crowd* by Thomas Hardy. There is a particular instance where Bathsheba enters an old hall wherein she finds the men relaxing on a long form and a settle at the hall's far end. Liddy follows Bathsheba into the room, where it is to be announced that the bailiff is fired for thieving and that, rather than hire a new bailiff, Bathsheba will manage things herself. Hardy describes the scene in the following manner:

> She [Bathsheba] sat down at the table and opened the time-book, pen in her hand, with a canvas money-bag beside her. From this she poured a small heap of coin. Liddy chose a position at her elbow and began to sew, sometimes pausing and looking round, or, with an air of a privileged person, taking up one of the half-sovereigns lying before her, and survey it merely as a work of art, while strictly forbidding her countenance from expressing any wish to possess it as money.[24]

What Hardy does not say speaks volumes over what he does. For instance, Liddy is reduced to *mere appearance*. It is clear that Liddy in fact does wish to possess the half-sovereigns as money, she simply forbids herself from showing this desire outwardly, by the expression on her face. It is also apparent that the "air of a privileged person" evoked by Liddy is a façade. She is, plainly, a servant, whose "privilege" lies in her being able to wait on a person of *real* privilege, namely, Bathsheba, a woman of such privilege that she may announce to a group of men that no other man will come in to manage her affairs. This is a standard hierarchical structure, one that severely limits the ethical call.

I am reminded by this passage of an episode in my own life, which occurred while I was a student. I was contracted by a company outside Philadelphia to buy used books from students on a college campus that my employers could then re-sell for profit. To do this, I was given a large sum of money in cash, to the amount of $25,000. Now, I am in the position of Liddy. I have $25,000 cash that at the same time I do not have. It is not my money, and so, I can look at it as Liddy does, acknowledging the great advances I could make in my life if I could possess this large sum, yet never able to acknowledge my own perspective, always expected to be the "face" of my employers—the face of the privileged. Further, I must give my life to this sum of money while never receiving from the sum anything for my life. I mean, I am expected to protect this money, possibly die for it if a persistent and violent criminal were to rob me, yet at no time may I draw upon this money *for my life*. There is a complete asymmetry between myself and this responsibility that does not admit my perspective. I am "privileged" to have this money, but only at the service of those with the real privilege of profiting from this sum. Now I was paid for my service, as Liddy makes a living at the service of Bathsheba, but I am always placed in an unethical stance. I cannot be honest about my feelings regarding this money; I must lie to myself and my employers and anyone else who would inquire about the money. Further, I am expected to be responsible for this money without ever taking responsibility for it. I cannot decide how to use the money, whether or not the prices I am paying for books is a fair price, whether or not the ultimate profit made on these books is in fair proportion to the cost of acquiring them. I cannot ask any of these questions. I am "the employee" and my possibilities are drastically curtailed by my submission to the contract.

I bring these less dramatic examples to light only to point to the subtle ways in which objectification can undermine our ethical encounters. It also speaks to the ways in which certain views of the self have become innocuously pervasive in our society, so much so that they are tacitly assumed in the writing of contracts and in the expectations placed on employees by their employers. I am not writing an outright polemic, only asking us to draw these everyday encounters into our critical analysis. An article by Kristen Munroe provides excellent historical evidence for these considerations. She writes:

> Instead, [of an agonistic choice between self and others] rescuers [of Jews during the Holocaust] operated out of a sense of the self in relation to others, suggesting that identity sets limits on the choice options perceived as available. The analysis thus suggests that moral theory needs to include not just identity, but also the relational aspect of identity. We need to allow for the critical ways in which our perspective on self in relation to others explains shifts in ethical action.[25]

RECAPITULATION

In *Black Boy*, Wright is repeatedly the victim of what has been called a "dark ontology." Charles Mills describes Enlightenment ontology, which is an ontology of the Same, as "dark" in three ways:

> First, it is dark in the sense of being color-coded, consigning non-whites to a lower rung on the ontological ladder. Second, it is dark in the sense of being sinister, a social ontology of domination and subordination. And finally, it is dark in the sense of being largely unacknowledged in Western political theory.[26]

A dark ontology is simply a special kind of negative ontology that is implicitly unethical. It carries the reduction of the I through to ends that are unethical, possibly immoral. To argue against this claim would be to define the abovementioned treatment of Richard Wright, and his subsequent dismissal from employment, as ethical, a controversy I will not encourage by entertaining as a possibility. My ultimate critique of analytic philosophies of personal identity arrives from the ethical perspective. I have shown through what methods reduction opens us to violence and given a lively illustration of actualized violence committed in terms of objectification. In relating the experience of a person victimized in such a way, we have again found a connection to the absurd. Wright's description of his walking down Capitol Street is a description of feeling the absurdity of one's situation. He must compare himself as nothing in the face of an authority that is everything. Stripped of his humanity, authority demands he be human, and thus have already condemned him to the worse guilt. He is, after all, just a nigger, and that judgment is the face of annihilating violence.

Given such an outcome negative ontologies must be abandoned, but to abandon them is to, along with Wright and Irigaray, wage a rebellion against our philosophical prejudices, which operate in terms of the Same as opposed to the Other. It is through the pursuit of this rebellion that theories of self will become "scientific." As it stands, especially in the case of reductionism, there is no hope of scientific rigor as long as the differentiation of subjectivity is ignored; what I mean is, as long as the *facts* of our own selves remain unacknowledged in difference to an ideal self that is only a sign. What we are currently working with is a calculus without the infinitesimal differentiation of the integral, with each person as an integral. Humanity rests on the infinite possibility of differentiation within a finite set of individuals.

INFINITY AND ALTERITY

We are now prepared for the Fourth Study, concerning an affirmative ontology. Before we embark on the final approach to our conclusion, I must insist on the relevancy of the idea of infinity to our current undertaking. Previously, I had discussed about every major philosopher of the Modern Period accept Leibniz. His formalization of differential calculus will at once demonstrate both the rigor and the utility of the idea of the infinite and prove with little effort the importance of the infinite to practical reason.

At first, it may not be precisely clear to those foreign to mathematical thinking how calculus could possibly relate to the current work. The "fundamental principle of the calculus" is defined by Leibniz as being: "Differences and sums are the inverses of one another, that is to say, the sum of the differences of a series is a term in the series, and the differences of the sums of a series is a term of the series," and these are expressed in Leibniz's notation as $\int dx = x$, and $d \int x = x$ respectively.[27] But as we follow Leibniz's thinking, we see that he develops his thesis to account for the *differences of the differences*. What develops is a way in which we can account for *any* possible point on a line, as well as on a curve, and as such are in a position to account for an apparently infinite number of variables. To do this we take three coordinates one of which remains constant while the other two continually approach the first until they simultaneously coincide with it.[28] Any difference of any other difference can thus be calculated by plotting points along the resulting figure. The relevance of these mathematical insights to the current study rests in the underlying logic of personal identity theories. The entire debate over personal identity concerned one constant variable (the self) and two other variables (physical and psychological criterion) that continually approached the first (from the past) until they simultaneously coincide with the constant variable (i.e. were identical with the self). Thus, it is a set of relations that define the outcome and the process of determination is relative to its end. The possible variables which would determine any calculation is an open set.

However, this is not the only insight to be gained from a mathematical metaphor. For instance, if any point on the number line can be accounted for, then any *indeterminate* point may also be accounted for, such as one *infinitesimally close to zero*, or any irrational, imaginary number resulting from a bizarre fraction, or π.

The possibilities become endless under the new calculus and we are opened to new ways of determining the area of a curved space, as well as for determining moments of a curve by a quadrature relative to *any arbitrarily produced* (or imagined) curve in the vicinity of the first. Leibniz can now talk about indeterminate variables in reference to the relations that hold between them. Indeterminate objects now take on relational definitions within the calculus that do not force them into an estimated determinate integer that expresses an error. The project of this thesis has been precisely to come to a relational understanding of an indeterminate entity without doing violence to that entity by reducing it into something it is not and thus invoking a grave error into our reasoning; collapsing the self into the mere reference of the sign that stands for it. An interesting way to think about this is to consider Leibniz's early acceptance of the Cartesian definition of a circle as a polygon with an infinite number of sides. In this way, each moment on a curve, as determined by a tangential calculation, becomes an infinitesimal side of the polygon, but is, more importantly, used to treat cycloids and pendulums.[29] But the circle, whose circumference consists in a curve, will not admit to a totalization of its sides, we can only talk about a determined number or none of them at a time and cannot tally them to a sum less than infinite. In truth, the circle is an indeterminate polygon.

It is the idea of infinity that will help us to do this effectively by directing our thinking toward a foundational alterity in which we are active participants. Moreover, it will help to achieve a heightened sense of rigor[30] in which we are not ignorant of the very real indeterminacy of certain entities in the world.

Notes to the Fourth Study

[1] William Faulkner, *Go Down, Moses*, (New York: Vintage International, 1990), 162.

[2] John Locke, *An Essay Concerning Human Understanding*, (Amherst, NY: Prometheus Books, 1995); 246—47.

[3] Ibid, 254.

[4] These points are elucidated to my satisfaction in Raymond Martin, "Locke's Psychology of Personal Identity." *Journal of the History of Philosophy* 38:1 (January 2000); 41—61.

[5] Bernard Williams, "The Self and the Future." *The Philosophical Review* 79:2 (Apr., 1970), 161.

[6] Locke, *An Essay Concerning Human Understanding*, 248.

[7] Ibid. 250—51.

[8] Robert Nozick, "Personal Identity Through Time." *Blackwell Readings in Philosophy: Personal Identity*, (Malden, MA: Blackwell Publishing, 2003), 97.

[9] A lengthy section of his 1984 book, *Reasons & Persons*, is devoted to this project of marginalizing personal identity, supposedly for the sake of ethical concerns. [Derek Parfit, "Part Three: Personal Identity." *Reasons & Persons*, (Oxford: Oxford University Press, 1987); 199—347.] He, like his predecessors, relies heavily on thought experiments to prove his dubious Reductionist thesis; the reasons for this will be explored in time.

[10] David Hume, *Treatise of Human Nature*, ed. L. A. Shelby-Bigge, (Oxford: Clarendon Press, 1896), 262.

[11] Derek Parfit, *Reasons and Persons*, 262.

[12] Levinas, *Totality and Infinity*, 92.

[13] For a full commentary, see: Michael J. MacDonald, "Losing Spirit: Hegel, Levinas, and the Limits of Narrative." *Narrative* 13:2 (May 2005); 182—94.

[14] Locke, *An Essay Concerning Human Understanding*, 255—6.

[15] Ibid, 256.

[16] This is laid out thoroughly in Immanuel Kant, "Transcendental Doctrine of Elements" in *Critique of Pure Reason*, trans. Norman Kemp Smith, (New York: Palgrave MacMillan, 2007); 65—570.

[17] Christine Korsgaard, "Personal Identity and the Unity of Agency: A Kantian Response to Parfit." *Philosophy and Public Affairs* 18:2 (1989), 109—23.

[18] Kant, *Critique of Pure Reason*, 169.

[19] Hegel, *Phenomenology of Spirit*, 36—7.

[20] Luce Irigaray, "The Question of the Other." *Yale French Studies* 87, *Another Look, Another Woman: Retranslations of French Feminism* (1995), 7.

[21] Ibid, 8. A translators note suggests "another subject" or "a subject which is other" as possible meanings.

[22] Ricoeur, *Oneself as Another*, trans. Kathleen Blamey, (Chicago: University of Chicago Press, 1992); 2—3.

[23] Richard Wright, *Black Boy*, (New York: Harper Perennial Modern Classics, 2006), 190. The subsequent events discussed in this section are described in Ibid; 188—94.

[24] Thomas Hardy, *Far From the Madding Crowd*, (Mineola, NY: Dover Publications, 2007), 67.

[25] Kristen Monroe, "How Identity and Perspective Constrain Moral Choice." *International Political Science Review/Revue internationale de science politique* 24:4 (Oct. 2003), 409.

[26] *Blackness Visible*, (New York: Cornell University Press, 1998), 74.

[27] Leibniz, "Undated Manuscript, Circa 1680." *The Early Mathematical Manuscripts of Leibniz*, trans. J. M. Child, (Derby: Merchant Books, 2007), 142.

[28] Leibniz, "Reply to Nieuwnetijt: Undated." *Early Manuscripts*, trans. J. M. Child; 156—7.

[29] Leibniz, "Reply to Nieuwnetijt," 149.

[30] Leibniz's use of infinitesimals is much elaborated upon and formalized by the work of later mathematicians such as Weierstrauss, Maltsev, Robinson, Nelson, and Hrbacek. Unfortunately, their concerns far outstrip the topics of the current thesis.

Fifth Study: Openness and Alterity

It could be said that this is merely a representation, a presentation, a manner of speaking an image or schema of the imagination in view of the idea of equality and in view of responding to the obligation attached to it, responding to it and answering for it responsibly.[1]

PREPARATION OF THE PHENOMENOLOGY OF THE PRECIPICE

The infinite is a relation of openness, not only metaphorically, but practically—to account for the experience of indeterminate phenomena. When Descartes instills the idea of the infinite at the basis of his epistemology, he creates a metaphysical façade out of a practical concept. It is the practical applications of the infinite that intrigue Leibniz, just as it had intrigued Archimedes and Zeno in antiquity.[2] Indetermination alone fails to account for the fullness of the implications of the infinite. The phenomenology of my encounter on the precipice will offer us a more robust account of this idea of the infinite, and thereby of myself, the true object of this inquiry. It will be shown in what ways I do and do not stand "at the center" of this phenomenology. This center is a center of perspective that is continually de-centered by the movement demarcated in previous studies, the movement that carries the self away from itself in the direction of itself. The preceding studies have prepared the way for this work. For one, they have offered critiques of both an ontology based on the primacy of presence (in the Third Study) and an ontology founded on separation and Sameness (in the Fourth Study). Such critiques have gained us enough intellectual distance to attempt, at least temporarily, the phenomenological bracketing of the theoretical. Once the phenomenology of my encounter on the precipice has been elucidated, I will enter the hermeneutic phase of the current Study, interpreting our critical philosophy through the relations described in the phenomenology.

THE PHENOMENOLOGY OF THE PRECIPICE

On the precipice, my relation to the horizon is a relation of profound openness—but profound in what sense? Profundity demarcates a depth, an intensity, a strong, imposing perception that requires an effort to understand. The struggle, the reemergence of $ἀλήθεια$, denotes a problematization of my being on the precipice. My openness is not merely a portal into the world. It is not merely a porthole through which I direct an intentional gaze out into the world. My gaze is always already in the world. The horizon disrupts this gaze and denies it the totalizing function of seeing the horizon itself. I do not see the horizon and know it. The horizon is that indeterminacy at which I can see no farther. In this sense it is a limitation. But this limitation is not a restriction that binds and closes upon me; it is rather synonymous with my situated openness. This horizon is the infinite distance made concrete. However I approach the horizon, this indeterminacy recedes from me as I approach it so that the relation between the horizon and myself is maintained without destroying the distance, and my traversing the distance does not destroy the relation. If I make a move toward the horizon, if I abandon the precipice and say, "I will see what is beyond the horizon," I have assumed a limit. This limit is differentiated from the horizon as something toward which I can move and move beyond. The horizon is not this beyond, nor is it that toward which I move. In my approach to the limit, the horizon recedes before me and offers to me, opens to me, presents to me the possibility of another beyond and still another beyond beyond that which was previously beyond. My relation is maintained in each of these movements beyond, and this transcendence of the limit is never a transgression of the horizon; it is the opening of the horizon.

Thus, the horizon, presented as the circumference of my perception, represented as a circle in which I stand, is the symbolic circle whose circumference is nowhere. Where is this horizon that I cannot meet, that recedes before me even as I approach so that I am thrown always back into a centrality that is decentralized by my movement? I struggle only when I identify my limit with horizon. I have set the limit; I cannot set the horizon. The horizon is always that beyond which signals transcendence to me. The horizon orients me towards transcendence.

This brings me to the great height that provides the vantage of the precipice. When we mention struggle, we must not mark this struggle as a purely negative phenomenon. I struggle up the mountain to reach the precipice. But my struggle is undertaken as one I accept. There is, in the very ascent, the implication of my acceptance. I say "yes" to the upward struggle knowing that this height awaits me. I climb. I ascend and when I reach the precipice it is reached as a pinnacle. I have then attained the perspective that opens me to the horizon in all of the ways previously mentioned. The idea of the infinite, which the horizon invokes in me, comes only after this struggle upward wherein the horizon is concealed by the mountainside rising before me. Once the precipice is approached, the horizon is revealed as this mingled indeterminacy; that is, of the earth and sky, and again, of Totality and Infinity. My acceptance of this struggle, my undertaking the climb with a sense of enjoyment, makes bearable the violence associated with struggle. I do not struggle with the mountain in order to dominate, this I cannot do, and how could I? My acceptance of this struggle is an acceptance of the mountain's place before me and of the height it opens to me, presents to me, gives to me freely, yet I must meet it, reach out to it in order to take the gifts of this height. The struggle is only a struggle to meet the mountain, to do my part in the offering of this height, in the maintenance of this profound openness. It is my responsibility.

This openness is something that must happen, that is to say, our historicity provides a context of openness—it is this openness that situates us not only toward the ethical, but an openness that, when closed upon, makes the unethical possible and is therefore openness to suffering as well as joy. Openness occurs existentially, giving only the trace of an essence that is thin as a veil.

There is an implied narrativity to the above phenomenology that results from coming to be on the precipice. I am not simply there on he precipice. My existence in this relation is not vacuous. I came to be on the precipice as a result of certain movements, upward movement for instance, or the struggle up the mountain. Thus I invoke some form of history on the precipice. I invoke time on the precipice. The relation to the horizon is temporally conditioned because my situation is not constant and the concretization of my relation to the horizon is not merely a matter of space, of physicality, or of materialistically constituted ontological schemes. The horizon is temporal as well as spatial. I move toward the horizon over time. My movement, by virtue of its temporality, becomes transitional only on the condition of this temporality that is constituted by a history that contextualizes me on the precipice. I approach hermeneutics.

The hermeneutic phenomenology presented by me as a description of the precipice is a manner of speaking about myself. But in the construction of this narrative I can only speak of myself in terms that do not reveal me as present. My presence is a presence in absentia. I am on the precipice only to the extent that I am not totalized by the horizon. My speaking is a speech delivered already after the fact of presence. My speech on the precipice, my calling out my name, or the utterance of any words echoed back to me from the landscape is a speech addressed to myself as another. I speak to hear myself speak but this speaking comes from a presence speaking to me in absentia. Why should I address myself if I am not involved with myself as another, if I am not at odds with the Other that is myself? What relation to the horizon do I have in solitude that is not a relation at once with myself? This temporalization must be addressed before we are able to move on the conclusive Study of the current work

A BEING IN TIME

To begin the hermeneutic process, I introduce the first line of *One Hundred Years of Solitude* by Gabriel García Márquez. He writes, "Many years later, as he faced the firing squad, Colonel Aureliano Buendía was to remember that distant afternoon when his father took him to discover ice."[3] The quotation opens us to a consideration of the multifarious nature of temporal theory. It is reminiscent of the equally famous first line of *Swann's Way* penned by Proust, which reads, "For a long time I would go to bed early."[4] *One Hundred Years of Solitude*, much like Proust's seven volume novel, is temporally complex. In the first line, Márquez indicates at least three different modes of temporality. There are, of course, the past, present, and future. But there is also ambiguity introduced through the theme of memory that disrupts the clarity with which the three times are referenced. As a result, we are not sure where the story begins. The origins become indeterminate. We begin in a "now," in the present of the line's deliverance. "Many years later..." seems to indicate many years from now, but this later is a moment of impending death. "Many years later, as he faced the firing squad..." Many years later the series of these years will come to an end, but from this limit we reach again into the past, to a discovery, to an uncovering. This past, through a statement in the present, has been drawn into a future by a memory invoked at the terminal moment. There is a "distance" that is bridged. Two afternoons are spanned, as two opposite shores are spanned, by the memory of an event that indicates historicity. I speak in the present of a future in which my past is present to my memory and thus represented in this future present as a past to which I am anchored in a concrete way. Márquez begins his novel on memory with a representation of representation itself. He shows me that I am not anchored by my spatiality. I am anchored by temporality as a boat is anchored to the depths. Spatiality gives up its secrets only over time and this time is plumbed as a depth from which I have attained height.

There exists a distance between me and myself that only temporality addresses. It is from this apparent multiplicity that the debate regarding personal identity over time emerges. Ought we really speak in terms of identity? Who is this Other to which I am identical then? If we give ourselves over to reductionism it cannot be me. But in this reduction I do violence to myself by the forceful separation of myself from my own identity. I am here *and* here…this plainly contradictory statement is alleviated by the refusal to confuse spatial language with temporal language. I am not "here and here" in time. I am now and then, etc. But is not this "now and then" precisely what is being accounted for by theories of personal identity? Perhaps, but it seems that the identity of persons over time cannot be construed *in terms of identity* simply because persons *are not substantially self-identical.* This self-identity is based on my presence in absentia. I confuse my speaking "I" with my real presence, which is never replicated in the signs of my language. I myself presuppose myself in order to deliver the sign that indicates myself, and thus, indication marks only a separation and not an identity. The identity of which the philosopher speaks is a formality rooted to a singularity that denotes itself through alterity. To be is to be other.

From the precipice, I repeat the steps taken toward the precipice through the precipitous acts of memory, which are, in their most robust formulation, the acts of narrativity. I open the vaults of my memory as a text emblazoned on the walls of an Egyptian tomb. Time may wear on these symbols and signs, but the rudimentary figures represented by memory harkens to me of the very experience that impressed the textual figure onto the wall. I speak metaphorically, of course, but below my metaphor lurks a deep and unavoidable phenomenon: those forever conjoined twins, memory and forgetting.

From the precipice, I read from myself as from a text, the text of my history, of my past, of my temporal relation to the horizon, which is not the ontological limitation of my being, but that very transcendence by which I go beyond this being, in which I relate to the Other, to alterity and to openness. Camus, in his incomplete final novel, speaks of this transcendence in the most visceral terms and brings us fully into the power of memory over the being that remembers and forgets. He writes of a character visiting the grave of the father he had never met, a father who had died young in a war far from home, far from a wife and son left to poverty and loneliness; loneliness born of forgetting. Camus writes:

> At that moment he read on the tomb the date of his father's birth, which he now discovered he had not known. Then he read the two dates, "1885—1914," and automatically did the arithmetic: twenty-nine years. Suddenly, he was struck by an idea that shook

his very being. He was forty years old. The man buried under this slab, who had been his father, was younger than he.

And the wave of tenderness and pity that at once filled his heart was not the stirring of the soul that leads the son to the memory of the vanished father, but the overwhelming compassion that a grown man feels for an unjustly murdered child…He looked at the other inscriptions in that section and realized from the dates that this soil was strewn with children who had been the fathers of graying men who thought they were living in this present time…All that was left was this anguished heart, eager to live rebelling against the deadly order of the world that had been with him for forty years, and still struggling against the wall that separated him from the secret of all life, wanting to go further, to go beyond, and to discover, discover at last in order to be, just once to be, for a single second, but forever.[5]

Like my struggle up the mountain, Camus' rebellion is not one of violent rejection, but one of acceptance, at last saying "yes" to that struggle that leads to this discovery; for Camus' character, the discovery of the secret of all life—of his whole life. The character had been estranged from his father, and his acceptance of his father coincides at last with this earth-shaking realization at the gravesite. This father, who had been denied for forty years, was now admitted and with this admittance comes a flood of experiential knowledge that consists of specifically temporal realizations. Time becomes necessary for transcendence.

Likewise, the relation to the other is not one of identity. It is a relation of necessity. To be, I need this other who is and is not myself, and these others from which I mark my separation as other. I am not determined ontically by otherness; rather, otherness constitutes the ontological determination of my being and this only after my being not-yet-present. Determination is a discovery made in hindsight, after a struggle against those theories that demand my contingency, that praise my irrelevance, and which sacrifice me as a lonely nothing to the machinery of Absurdity. I am thus freely anchored, or more accurately, anchored freely so that my contingency means only that I could always be other than what I happen to be at any given moment. But this contingency is not foundational.

FOUNDATIONAL ETHICS

The necessity of the Other is unveiled in the foundational nature, not of ontology, but of ethics. This is the sublime realization of Kant's critical philosophy. There are two ways of interpreting Kantian ontology, one of which is of far more use to me than the other. The basic Kantian understanding, which is to then be interpreted, involves the notion of space and time as mediums of experience, as those immediate structures *through which we experience the phenomenal world*.[6] According to Kantian terminology, space and time constitute the self-evident, already posited forms necessary to bring about perception. Without space and time, perception itself becomes impossible, left to "float" in a "void" of non-sensibility (even "float" and "void" constitute spatial and temporal concepts; according to Kant, I cannot express ideas without reference to space and time).

There are two ways this insight can be interpreted. One views space and time as limiting conditions of perception. Space and time create limits within which reason can function. Admittedly there is some textual evidence to support such an interpretation. Kant often refers to space and time as "necessary" and as "determining" perception in some way and, of course, as a "limitation."[7] But we must be careful in our examination of the text. A thorough reading reveals some interesting stipulations, introduced by Kant, that lift the notion of limitation from the functions of time and space in perception. A careful reading of the text will show these terms of limit to refer *back* to the concepts of space and time themselves, so that, rather than strictly limiting perception, space and time are limited to objective and subjective functionalities respectively. That functionality, rather than being limited, is instead described predominantly in terms of *possibility*, thus, of *openness*. Determinacy has taken on very specific meanings in twentieth century philosophy, especially among analytics of free will and moral responsibility. These more contemporary uses of determination were in all probability foreign to Kant's way of thinking, especially given his conclusion that questions concerning the freedom of the will were epistemologically untenable to say the least. The claim really seems to be that space and time are themselves limited to the objective and subjective spheres, they are not limitations of perception per se, they are the very possibility of perception in the first, *a priori*.

So the second interpretation, which I endorse here,[8] sees time and space not as limitations to our experience, but as our very openness to experience. Time and space do not determine us, rather, we determine time and space as *a priori* faculties of cognition. Time and space are enablers, they facilitate our perception of the world in all its possibilities so that limitation can be placed only on time and space itself, and then only provisionally. The measurement of time, the so-called objective nature of time, is only a limit set by us for practical purposes. In reality, objective time means only a series of spatial changes occurring in succession, the succession of which is intuited subjectively, since in the objective world the successive series is not spatially instantiated simultaneously. Experience seems to support Kantian theory, to a point. Thinkers such as Henri Bergson, William James, and Gilles Deleuze develop internalized theories of subjective time further, especially in Bergsonian and Jamesian treatments of "duration."[9] Of these thinkers, Deleuze does the most to break us out of the formal subject/object dichotomy.[10] However, for our current purposes, it does no good to continue to attach time and space to subjectivity and objectivity respectively, as Kant does. Instead, we must follow a different path, one opened by the persistent critique of the subject/object dichotomy itself, as we have followed it in the work of Heidegger. Unlike Heidegger, we will see that this path leads us not to ontology, but to ethics as the foundational characteristic of being, or of what it means to be.

Phenomenologically, following Heidegger, when we direct our intentionality at something in order to "grasp" it or understanding it, we do not first pass from some "inner sphere," in which we are enclosed, into an objective world that is "outside" of cognition. Rather, we are always already in the world alongside the objects we wish to grasp, already in a world discovered.[11] When this assertion is upheld, the dichotomy between space and time, formerly supported by the subject/object dichotomy, dissolves and the Kantian stipulations on the limitations of the transcendental aesthetics breaks up into a function of mediation. This mediation is to be sought in alterity.

We must be careful when treating *Dasein* not to reduce *Dasein* to an impersonal formulation of what is immanently personal, dooming it to the critiques formulated in earlier Studies. A foundational ontology cannot be an ontology of negation, dissolving along with the subject the persons to whom the subjectivity was formerly attributed. But neither does authentic *Dasein* appear human in the full sense of the word. *Dasein* may stand for existence, abstractly construed, it but does not take nourishment from the tools it engages. We pick up on Levinas' criticism of Heidegger. For Levinas, what Heidegger describes in terms of equipment are those things in the world through which we live, through which life becomes livable. We take nourishment from these entities in the sense that we engage them fully and fulfill ourselves through actions and relationships that are enabled by the enjoyment of and participation in these "worlds," as Heidegger would call them.[12] *Dasein* is not fulfilled beyond the utilization of objects as equipment through which the world is revealed as one in which I am. When *Dasein* does not appear alongside the object, I am nowhere while the object reveals my embodiment only as another object in the scheme of utilization.

Ontically speaking, my body is utilized to engage equipment. Thus, in being ontological, I abscond from the ontic description of engagement when I move to being ontological so that, in my description, embodied *Dasein* appears as an object in the world alongside other objects.

At this point the former problems of embodiment, which Heidegger works very hard to eliminate, reappear in his transition to ontological descriptions of ontic characteristics. However, I am not this object that is just another alongside objects in the world, but I am constituted in the difference of not being just one object among others, and yet, now seeing myself as just one object among others. I am not the object I see as being alongside others, and this being in the face of the others constitutes me as more than a mere object among others. Heidegger disrupts this cycle through ontology to the ontic by emphasizing touch, and this does much to alleviate the problems discussed so far. Our excess is the manifestation of an economy of being, of an active mediation of being through alterity. We must take care not to conflate Derrida's treatment of "economy" with that of Levinas', for the two do not share the same insight regarding economy and excess.[13] When Derrida opposes economy and excess, he does so in terms of an "economy of violence." For Levinas, this violence already denotes a totality in and from which there is inclusion and exclusion. Therefore, when I talk about excess—here outstripping the totality and totalizing functions—I am entering into an economy that need not be violent in which the mediation between the other and myself can be an ethical relation, which the economy of violence seems to preclude.[14] There, myself and the other, beyond the totality, constituted in excess of the totality, enter the totality *against* violence for justice; thus the economy formed need not be *on the basis of violence* but *on the basis of peace*—a possibility of which Derrida is highly skeptical. When dealing with Levinas on economy, we must be careful of the third party, and even more careful not to read "third party" as an entity, even as society, constituted outside the other and myself. Levinas says, quite elegantly, that:

> [The] entry of the third party is the *very fact of consciousness*, assembling into being, and at the same time, in a being, the hour of suspension of being in possibility, the finitude of essence accessible to the abstraction of concepts, to the memory that assembles in presence, the reduction of a being to the possible and the reckoning of possibles, the comparison of incomparables. It is the thematization of the same on the basis of the relationship with the other, starting with proximity and the immediacy of saying prior to problems, whereas the identification of knowing by itself absorbs every other.[15]

And so, the third party is not some entity over and above myself and the other, or myself as another. It is the very description of this relationship within the totality, within the totality now opened to peace and justice. The economy of being is ethics and is the foundation of our being in the world. Thus we see again that ethics precedes ontology.[16]

FORGETTING REMEMBERING TRUTH

Earlier, I had mentioned "forever conjoined twins, memory and forgetting." I have, however, put forgetting first in the section heading above in order to introduce an important relationship between forgetting, memory, and truth that has been implicitly maintained by the hermeneutic nature of the current work. It has been suggested by László Tengelyi that "A hermeneutic phenomenology necessarily vindicates *truth* for poetic language and art. However, whereas truth is *learned* from scholarly books, it is *experienced* in art and literature, just as in life."[17] To a great extent, the critical sections of the current work have been concerned with attempting to forget the learned scholarly opinion regarding selfhood in order to meet the phenomenology of the precipice without the blinders of philosophical prejudice. It is by this forgetting, itself largely metaphorical, for what is learned is not entirely forgotten: it is recast, redescribed, and born again, this time in a new light. In this way, we remember truth, so to speak. This is not to endorse a Socratic understanding of knowledge as recollection. Of course, I am speaking of remembering truth as the recollection of an experience of truth—of actual lived experience. In the theoretical, we often forget the actual experience that engages us, or rather, that we engage in, everyday. It is the everyday experience that Heideggerian analysis of *Dasein* attempts to address.

So we avoid an impersonal interpretation of *Dasein* by remembering the special privilege of *touch* in *Being and Time*. Touch is characteristic of *Dasein*. Nothing else touches in the sense that I can reach out and touch an entity in the world. Of course, the additional fact that I can reach out and touch *someone*, some other, adds another emphasis, especially considering, as we have, the work of Levinas.[18] And so I want to emphasize, along with

Ricoeur,[19] a positive description of memory as a characteristic, similar to touch, of the I, especially in the capacity of being *ontische ontologische*. I remember, and I forget. At times, I remember what I had forgotten, which is different, perhaps, from remembrance, or again, of commemoration. There is an Honor of being human that we are commemorated, not only by different memories of ourselves at once, but of various memories of others at different times still. And forgetting is not only being forgotten. Sometimes, these memories are enhanced by omissions, but not erasures. Events are not erased, and often even the memories of events are not erased from consciousness. Instead, forgetting can actively serve as a kind of forgiveness, or in the mode of forgiving. Sometimes, in order to forgive, I forget a certain significance, deemed offensive, once attached to the act, to the actual, and my forgiveness obscures this former significance. The offensive significance is rendered null by a forgetting that informs future acts toward this other whom we are said to forgive. Forgiveness is but one of the gifts of forgetting.

This absolution obtains on the condition that this forgetting is remembered. That is to say, that we honor the obligation promised by this forgiving qua forgetting, which is never a "pure" or Absolute forgiveness. I forget as a gift to the other and remember this gift for the other. Memory keeps and disrupts order, and this is the relation to truth, to truth in the sense that I accept a given interpretation as a history I can reconcile myself to. Indeed, the truth is a thematization I can exist within peaceably, without violence. It may possibly be a just objectification. Truth is then ambivalently connected to justice, to some value thematized as being "good," even when we speak of "objective truth," for this judgment precedes the very act of seeking this truth, of undertaking the struggle presented by ἀλήθεια. How easily truth and justice are insinuated together as fortuitous bedfellows. Truth is presented and represented by what is "right," a forcefully ambiguous word, and the rightness of truth points us directly toward the justice of truth that presents to us, by its historicity, the culmination of ἀλήθεια in the achievement of knowledge. Epistemologically, I can only be said to know according to certain functions of memory, keeping in order a certain set of claims regarding corresponding experiences over time. Temporality, again, implies active mnemonic existence. The full significance of Márquez's beautiful opening lines is becoming clear. They recall for us the experience of the narrative truth of our lives; that we experience this temporal arc that has lead to a certain terminus, for Aureliano Buendías, to the firing squad. But we are also surprised!

Surprised that when the firing squad takes aim at Colonel Aureliano Buendías

> ...the rage had materialized into a vicious and bitter substance that put his tongue to sleep and made him close his eyes. Then the aluminum glow of dawn disappeared and he saw himself again in short pants, wearing a tie around his neck and he saw his father leading him into the tent on a splendid afternoon, and he saw the ice. When he heard the shout he thought that it was the final command to the squad. He opened his eyes with a shudder of curiosity, expecting to meet the incandescent trajectory of the

bullets, but he only saw Captain Roque Carnicero with his arms in the air and José Arcadio crossing the street with his fearsome shotgun ready to go off.

"Don't shoot." The captain said to José Arcadio.

"You were sent by Divine Providence."[20]

And so we discover that Buendías is granted a reprieve, and we are left to learn it with him, as the character himself learns that he will live beyond his execution. This is jarring news to the character, and psychologically compelling to me as a reader. I feel this alarm, this surprise at being. We can surprise ourselves. Given the historicity of our narrative such surprises are not arbitrary. For our context to be intelligible, it must be comprehensible and expresses the experiential aspect of truth when we are said to intuit what is so when it is well established.[21] The same can be said of speech derived from prejudice, and here again reflection and $\dot{\alpha}\lambda\acute{\eta}\theta\varepsilon\iota\alpha$ as "unconcealedness" reemerge. We must work toward truth, much as we work toward our conclusion.

RECAPITULATION

The phenomenology of the precipice has described the relation of the I to the horizon as one of openness. It has been shown throughout in what ways saying "I" is only a manner of speaking, only a way of saying "Soul," *cogito*, "Ego," "Spirit," "Self," etc. These are signs I signal myself by, but I am not the sign I signal myself by. To account for this, temporality has been addressed and given a robust role that, unfortunately, cannot be more fully expounded upon. Such a discourse is worthy of future attention; however, the needs of the current analysis were addressed and meet with the rigor appropriate to them.

Temporality, understood according to the above analysis, points us toward the horizon as a transcendent relationship. The transcendent has put us on course to lay a foundational ethic, better, to put ethics as the first philosophy. Levinas writes that, "Already *of itself* ethics is an 'optics'."[22] By this, we are to understand that ethics is not limited to a theoretical ordering of thought which prescribes a method, or system by which a person can be ethical, or as part of the religious in Levinas' thought, to be in relation to the transcendent. Ethics is a way we see the transcendent, a way we see and hear the other and which leads us to the other, by which we reach out and touch the other. Levinas uses the metaphor of ethics as a road here, as well as the metaphor of vision, which is classically a metaphor of truth. Considering narrative under a literary model, using appropriate analogies between text and context, a positive account of memory and forgetting have illuminated an experiential perspective on truth, which is consistent with the hermeneutic phenomenology undertaken in the previous Studies. The overall discussion has drawn into focus the key points derived from the previous chapters, and prepared us, at last, for the concluding Study of the work. In order to do this, we must first draw from the preceding remarks a definite expression of Otherness, a term left to obscurity by the First Study.

OTHERNESS

It has been shown in many ways how I am other to myself. The Other, as that which is Absolutely Other, is constitutive of the Infinite. And so, this other who is myself is analogous to the idea of the infinite in us, as a representation of ourselves in terms of that Other who we meet in the transcendent relation. Here I must address the face-to-face encounter, because this is really what I mean by the transcendent relation, and, I believe, what Levinas meant by it also. "The face to face is a final irreducible relation which no concept could cover without the thinker who thinks that concept finding himself forthwith before a new interlocutor; it makes possible the pluralism of society."[23] Just as the Other is irreducible, I too am irreducible to some concept or sign or symbol. But I am not this infinite for myself, and do not represent this Other to myself as the other does. In the face of the other, I experience the radical separation from the Other that left Descartes unable to speak of anything more than the *idea of the infinite in me*. Being mediated to myself qua otherness only instigates a cycle that the other breaks and disrupts. Myself as the other is an ethical relation to myself *as to another*. Rather than an ethics of egoism, I am opened to a startlingly altruistic ethics wherein my egoism is but the mimicry of my obligation to the other. My own self-immanence comes to me only through this other that is myself. My Otherness is at once my openness unto the world, is my relation to that horizon as transcendence. There is the key to the gift of presence on the precipice. This was the elusive subject of our Studies. In the perpetual transition suggested by temporality, we are never alone. Stranded in the presence of the other, I am only because we are. This is not a paradox, and we shall conclude with this expression, its various philosophical manifestations.

Notes to the Fifth Study

[1] Jacques Derrida, *The Politics of Friendship*, trans. George Collins, (New York: Verso, 2005), 262.

[2] Archimedes developed a very archaic method of infinitesimals in order to calculate measurements of the Earth's surfaces, and was essential to Leibniz's formulation of the "Characteristic Triangle," that is, an indeterminate triangle (being infinitely small). See Leibniz, "Historia et Origo." *The Early Mathematical Manuscripts of Leibniz*, trans. J. M. Childs, (Derby: Merchant Books, 2007), 38. Zeno's famous paradoxes are but practical defenses of Parmenides' theory of the One. Zeno seems to think that, practically speaking, if the space between two points can be divided infinitely then we can never traverse that distance. See Kathleen Freeman, "Zeno of Elea." *Ancilla to the Pre-Socratic Philosophers*, (Cambridge: Harvard University Press, 1983), 47. Leibniz's calculus takes the practicality of this reasoning further by assuming the fact that we do indeed traverse distances that are infinitely divisible.

[3] Gabriel García Márquez, *One Hundred Years of Solitude*, trans. Gregory Rabassa, (New York: Harper Perennial Modern Classics, 2006), 1.

[4] Marcel Proust, *In Search of Lost Time Vol. 1: Swann's Way*, trans. C. K. Scott Moncrieff & Terence Kilmartin, (New York: The Modern Library, 2003), 1.

[5] Albert Camus, *The First Man*, trans. David Hapgood, (New York: Vintage International, 1996); 25—7.

[6] "Time is the formal *a priori* condition of all appearances whatsoever. Space, as the pure form of all outer intuition, is so far limited; it serves as the *a priori* condition only of outer appearances." Kant, *Critique of Pure Reason*, trans. Norman Kemp-Smith, (New York: Palgrave MacMillan, 2007), 77.

[7] Ibid; 67, 68, 72 & 74.

[8] In this interpretation I follow Otfired Höffe, *Immanuel Kant*, trans. Marshall Farrier, (Albany, NY: SUNY Press, 1994); 56—59, 63.

[9] See: Henri Bergson, *Matter and Memory*, trans. Nancy Margaret Paul & W. Scott palmer, (New York: Zone Books, 2005); 185—6, 205—13. See also: William James, "From *The Principles of Psychology*." *The Essential Writings*, ed. Bruce W. Wilshire, (Albany, NY: SUNY Press, 1984); 119—27.

[10] For the relevance of his thought to the problems of time currently under discussion, see: Gilles Deleuze, *Difference and Repetition*, trans. Paul Patton, (New York: Columbia University Press, 1994); 85—91.

[11] The preceding two sentences serve as a very loose translation, really more of a summation, of the following passage: *Im Sichrichten auf... und Erfassen geht das Dasein nicht etwa erst aus seiner Innensphäre hinaus, in die es zunächst verkapselt ist, sondern es ist seiner primären Seinsart Nach Immer schon »draußen« bei einem begegnenden Seienden der je schon untdeckten Welt.* Heidegger, *Sein und Zeit*, (Tübingen: Max Niemeyer, 1967), 62.

[12] Levinas, *Totality and Infinity*, trans. Alfonso Lingis, (Pittsburgh: Duquesne University Press, 1969); 127—30.

[13] This point is argued in Martin Hägglund, "The Necessity of Discrimination: Disjoining Levinas and Derrida." *Diacritics* 34.1, 40—71.

[14] In doing this, I follow Levinas' discussion of "economic relations" carried on in "The *I* and Totality." *Entre Nous: Thinking-of-the-other*, trans. Michael B. Smith & Barbara Harshav, (New York: Continuum Press, 2006); 11—33.

[15] Levinas, *Otherwise than Being*, trans. Alphonso Lingis, (Pittsburgh: Duquesne University Press, 1998), 158.

[16] This is an argument key to understanding the work of Emmanuel Levinas. See: Levinas, "Is Ontology Fundamental?" *Entre Nous: Thinking-of-the-other*, trans. Michael B Smith & Barbara Harshav, (New York: Continuum Press, 2006); 1—10.

[17] L. Tengelyi, "Redescription and Refiguration of Reality in Ricoeur." *Research in Phenomenology* 37 (2007), 164.

[18] See: Heidegger, *Being and Time*, trans. MacQuarrie & Robinson, (New York: HarperCollins, 1962); 79—80.

[19] Ricoeur writes, "of a warning against the tendency of many authors to approach memory on the basis of its deficiencies, even its dysfunctions...It is important...to approach the description of mnemonic phenomena from the standpoint of the *capacities*, of which they are the "happy" realization." Paul Ricoeur, *Memory History Forgetting*, trans. Kathleen Blamey & David Pellauer, (Chicago: Chicago University Press, 2006), 21.

[20] Márquez, *One Hundred Years of Solitude*, 128—29.

[21] "Truth is in effect not separable from intelligibility; to know is not simply to record, but always to comprehend. We also say that to know is to justify, making intervene, by analogy with the moral order, the notion of justice." Levinas, *Totality and Infinity*, 82.
[22] Ibid, 29.
[23] Ibid, 291.

Concluding Study: I Am Because We Are

I am because we are; and since we are, therefore I am.[1]

WISDOM FROM THE CRADLE OF HUMANITY

I first encountered the phrase "I am because we are" as the title of an anthology of black philosophy edited by Fred Lee Hord (Mzee Lasana Okpara) and Jonathan Scott Lee. This anthology was the result of a team-taught course offered by the two editors on black philosophy, an important and controversial course in philosophy at the time of the anthology's publication in 1995. Up to that time, the general consensus seemed to be that there simply *was no* black philosophy, the result of dark ontology as noted in the Fourth Study. Hord and Lee, however, shared and voiced the conviction that there was, to quote:

> …a source of wisdom in the work of certain black philosophers that might prove quite valuable in rethinking the lives of individuals in Western societies and in provoking philosophical critiques of the subtle (an not-so-subtle) effects of colonialist and

neocolonialist thinking on issues of personal identity and community.[2]

Later, I discovered a variation on this marvelous theme in the work of a different sort of African, who proclaimed in the language of colonizers, *"Sur cette limite, le « Nous sommes » définit paradoxalement un nouvel individualisme."*[3] It was then, reading Camus, that I realized the historical depth of Hord and Lee's insight. In fact, the thought of black Africans had already begun to take firm hold on the thinking of the West. It was particularly prevalent among those who were searching for new expressions of community and individualism in the aftermath of the two World Wars and who faced the consequences of colonialism first hand, often from a perspective of historical exile. This is an exile wherein the individual is exiled at home, a home forged by foreigners among natives who, while refusing to become like the natives, nevertheless produced sons and daughters who felt themselves natives in their own right. Here I imagine Camus' condition as an inversion of Richard Wright in *Black Boy*. What I mean is this: Camus is manifestly the Same, the white European male. He could be seen as an example of the oppressor class. However, it is this Sameness that Camus rejects in his rebellion, a rebellion we can now see is shared with Wright. Whereas Wright was in the United States, was a "native" of the U.S. and found himself marginalized as the "other" in that society, Camus was born in Algeria, where Islamic Algerian revolutionaries saw him as the oppressor, even despite the often-extreme poverty in which Camus was raised. Camus' paradoxical new individualism is an individualism dependent on the community from which it springs, and is therefore in complete recognition of the Otherness of each individual. The Same has been overthrown in *The Rebel* in exchange for a centralized otherness that speaks to me as I am, that is as a singularity not the Same, irreducible to the Same, to whom violence is done in this very reduction to the Same.

It is true that Camus does not give credit to the African tradition whose formulation of "I am because we are" is at the core of his new individualism. But it is also true that traditional Africans did not formulate their communitarian proverb from the perspective of individualism, which provided the intellectual context wherein Camus wrote. Further, it is against this strict individualism that Camus argues for the dignity and value inherent in human life, in living itself. And so he is in agreement with the ancient Egyptian teachings of Ptahhotep proclaiming that "To see everyone is to satisfy the many. Any riches that you have are useless without the many."[4] We can see echoed too, from *The Declarations of Innocence* circa 1500 BCE, the proclamation, "Hail, Lord of faces, who comest forth from Netchfet, I have not judged hastily."[5] To meet the other in the face-to-face encounter is perhaps, above all, not to judge them hastily, to allow them to be without forcing the comparison to the Same to which they cannot measure up and from which each one is by definition excluded.

I have pursued a critique of my own prejudices and my own culture so that I might discover these wisdoms anew, so that I can read St. Augustine as a Christian, a Catholic, an African, a man, human, as he is on the page—Rational, irrational, confessing. But I also have undertaken this work so that I might understand why I am not a Christian, though I confer with Christians and commune with them in this historical time we share. Indeed, so that I might understand what philosophical atheism can mean for our identity if the historical accounts of our relation to the transcendent are denied, and that such a position is not absurd. So that I can say what atheism might mean, how the Absurd collapses in community, and in what ways I am this other of whom I have spoken at length. I begin my conclusions from here, from this sage wisdom from the cradle of humanity, as I have begun each new leg of this work. That is, from the origin, from an origin with which I share a few generative themes.

I must note a comment by Hord and Lee regarding generative themes in black philosophy. They claim that several "generative themes" in black philosophy result in the fact that:

> ...though themes may be common, the products that grow out of these themes—the texts and philosophies that sprout—will often be strikingly different. We do not intend these generative themes to serve as reductionistic specifications of the 'essence' of black philosophy we recognize in them, rather, the seeds from which an astonishing number of different gardens have grown.[6]

So that I might solidify the connection I point out these generative themes, all of which resonate in the current thesis. They are: 1) the idea that the identity of the individual is never separable from the sociocultural environment; 2) a fundamentally relational conception of reality; and 3) the central importance of religion and religion-based ethics as dominant forms for the fundamentally social expression of core philosophical ideas.[7] More on theme number 3 to come, for the form of my religious expression my very well be unrecognizable from the perspective of Hord and Lee's African worldview.[8]

The concluding study that follows serves as a summation of the central points proposed by the current work and attests most directly to those whose work has come before it. It also makes a few minor confessions that are intended to convey with honesty the general feelings that the previous studies have stirred in their author. However, emphasis lies here in summation and in making clear the conclusions we are to derive from the arguments preceding us. In brief, I am to explain how I am mediated always by otherness in the simplest terms thus far employed, and in doing so, will briefly outline how the door is to be closed on Absurdity and how the term "atheism" applies to my philosophy in general. By doing these two things in reference to the overall point of self-mediation through otherness, I am making a case for how the self is related to the world it finds itself in—the role of myself in the "grand scheme of things," so to speak.

On these points, the African's seem to stand with Levinas *against* the Heideggerian notion of *Mitsein* because, here at the ethical we find "the *Mitsein* in perpetual communion and perpetual vitality."[9] This quote from Joseph M. Nyasani comes from a thesis that is important for establishing what, for me at least, is a central insight of the current work; that is, "…my existence is not entirely my own nor can I perpetuate it in total disregard or defiance of others' concerns without incurring a damnation or actually losing some life-force."[10] On this point, I imagine taking nourishment from the others as Levinas sees us nourished by our engagement.

Nyasani points to some crucial questions regarding the "absorption" of the I into the We, but these concerns rest on an understanding of the I already drastically undermined by the preceding Studies. For me, the I has never really stood beyond the We in order that could be absorbed, rather, the I is always already absorbed and working within this community to uncover its relations. So:

> ...the individual exists not exclusively for himself but for others as well in the sense that his independent existence would be neither a reality nor a factor in the absence of concurrent forces of community. For in the community the individual can claim his individuality and personal autonomy.[11]

CLOSING THE DOOR ON ABSURDITY

We are not Absurd; though at times we are absurd. I have used the term "Absurd" to denote a fundamental relation between oneself and the rest of reality. That is that one is rendered essentially meaningless by the mechanisms of objective reality which will inevitably erase all trace of any person's existence from, not only history, but from the very face of reality. The fact of such erasure, supposing it is indeed a fact, is irrelevant to our ultimate meaning. It is not by some "intensity of thought and feeling," to return to the Bertrand Russell quotation cited in the First Study, that I hope to forcibly insert my life's meaning into a philosophical hypothesis. That would seem a vain, pseudo-philosophic assumption of great irony. It is rather by the sober realization that Russell can meaningfully refer us to a scale of intensity applicable to these very thoughts and feelings that shows him to be already entangled in a highly meaningful interpretative mode, only underscoring with the intensity of his own thought the very meaning he is condemning as ultimately irrelevant. Rarely has the deep meaning of our own meaninglessness been so passionately expounded. Or perhaps Russell himself is ironic.

See how he turns, in the end, to hope and a faith in hope, we find so often in the *religious* thinker:

> Be it ours to shed sunshine upon their [fellow men's] path, to lighten their sorrows by the balm of sympathy, to give them the pure joy of a never-tiring affection, to strengthen failing courage, to instill faith in hours of despair. Let us not weigh in grudging scales their merits and demerits, but let us remember that they are fellow sufferers in the same darkness, actors in the same tragedy with ourselves.[12]

And I thought we were to build on the rock of despair? Here we see foundations lay on a kernel of hope. Yet I sympathize and perhaps share in this with Camus, whose hope appeared a rock of its own, more robust and elegant in its emotive provocation. It was Camus' project, after all, to disprove the philosophic tenability of suicidal despair in the face of the Absurd. It is primarily the disintegration of the Absurd in the logic of *The Myth of Sisyphus* that the suicidal escape is discredited.

While the question of suicide is beyond my own project, I do affirm that the Self is a *meaningful being*. We exist in a world of meaning, so to speak. In previous studies I enter into conversation after conversation which are always already in progress. Thus I never arrive at anything like a historical root of the concepts singled out for philosophic inquiry. As such, the job of philosophy, specifically of philosophic hermeneutics, is to constantly re-open the questions in new ways derived from the multiplicity of interpretability. In short, words don't have one meaning and one meaning only, and this fact introduces, as a necessity for philosophic rigor, the need to analyze varying interpretations without those interpretations necessarily excluding one another. To be even more brief: avoid rigid dichotomies.

This again refers us to our openness. From here, we see that even "meaninglessness" is itself a meaning. I therefore, by the strange logic introduced by the meaningful/meaningless dichotomy applied to the meaning of life, find meaning in my very meaninglessness. My "purpose" then becomes not to mean; an absurdly negative imperative in which my very denial of meaning constitutes the context by which I mean. I intend to mean from my meaninglessness. I mean in meaninglessness. The erasure of my presence from existence is likened to the opening within an enclosure discussed in the Third Study. The past closes on me in the form of history, of what has happened, but my opening to the future is an opening *from the closure of the past*. The past closes, and I am opened to the future. So the past constitutes this opening into the future, and that "closedness" of the past is represented in the future as something determined from which something new can begin. All this closure amounts to is the consistent novelty of the present and the epistemological uncertainty of the future. We may "know" something about the future, but this "knowledge" is provisional given the novelty experienced in the present and anticipated in the future. Thus I can only be absurd as a contrivance, in humor or tragedy.

THE MEANING OF ATHEISM

The philosophy unfolding out of this initial rejection of the Absurd, which was given ground in the Third and Fourth Studies, and developed fully in the Fifth Study, is an atheist philosophy because the meaning of life is not contingent on God. The concept of the Divine is not necessary, under the current thesis, to provide me with identity, and thus with meaning, purpose, or dignity. In fact, unwavering faith in a certain conviction of God can be seen as an ethical hindrance if we accept the theory of personal identity under consideration. If we approach our engagement with the world as if our own judgments coincided with the Judgment of God (this coincidence due to our subscription to a particular religious creed or knowledge of certain texts) then there appears an exceptionally high probability that we will not see or engage others ethically. We will be quick to differentiate between sinners and saved, pious and heretical, Same and Other, Master and Slave, Black and White, *Brahmin* and Untouchable.

While I intend the prefix "a-" in "atheism" as a rejection of certain historical formulations of God as a concept, I must recognize and point out that the prefix "a-" has a great variety of applications beyond mere negation. From the Greek we get "not, without" and these already carry us beyond rejection. "Without" implies the exile from God imposed by Genesis, as discussed in the Second Study. But the subsequent development of the phenomenological account of the precipice in the Fifth Study grounds this mythological account of creation into the concrete relation between myself and the Other, and even myself who is that Other. The ethical consequences are then atheistic in the sense of being without God and take on a rather humanistic tone, this due largely to the perspective of philosophic anthropology, discussed in the First Study and prominent throughout the argumentation of the entire work. *Psuchē*, the Self, the ontological I, is grounded in the interrelation with the Other through which the I arrives at self-knowledge. The primary epistemological thrust of this essay has been that the I is mediated by otherness, mediated to itself and the other not by some principle of ideal Similarity, but on the basis of a radical Otherness that breaks consciousness from consistent thematization. Consistent, systematized interpretation is always drawn into question by the other's freedom, by their ability to surprise us, and by the possibility of violence resulting from objectification, or totalization, or sheer egoism. I have not attempted at any time to describe a law of being by which the I is. Rather, my argument is for a particular constitution of the I in a relational ontology that affirms the I as a locus of relations in the world. The relation to the horizon was put into focus, again, to describe a non-theistic relation to the transcendent that enabled a detailed analysis of alterity and openness lending a more robust account of the self's mediation through otherness. But this cannot appear as a system. As the Third Study affirmed, there is no end to the detour through the Other. This detour presents the constant re-opening of the ethical question by the arrival of the Self in the presence of the Other. Stranded in the presence of the Other, the questioning of our own being has always been the reference to an ethical stance. This stance has always been taken upon the rather personal and unquantifiable notion of some value, worth, dignity, or simple self-preservation that we see can now arise through a consciousness of otherness connecting us to and rooting us in (rooting us in the sense that we draw nourishment from) the others that bring me into relation with the Other.

The above conception and use of "atheism" has resonated quietly throughout the current work as the phrase "O my friends, there is no friend" resonated throughout Derrida's *The Politics of Friendship*.[13] We speak of God while denying the existence of God, forever wrestling the concept, the idea of the infinite in us, affirming at once while denying the very transcendent realized on the precipice. So we say, "O my God, there is no god" and are without God in the radical separation denoted by the transcendent. We may express a faith, and faith may constitute a philosophic aspect open to inquiry, and again, multiple interpretive accounts, but for ourselves it is not proper to say that God constitutes the grounding of our being, even in a theological context. The "We are" constitutes this groundedness, and from this has been derived the mediation qua the Other. Implied throughout the exposition of this mediation is a warning regarding the Same, not an outright condemnation, but the application of hermeneutics to the Same.

ESCHATOLOGICAL ETHICS: HERMENEUTIC RELIGION AND THE OTHER

Camus writes,

> Believe me, religions are on the wrong track the moment they moralize and fulminate commandments. God is not needed to create guilt or

> to punish. Our fellow men suffice, aided by ourselves. We were speaking of the Last Judgment…I shall wait for it resolutely, for I have known what is worse, the judgment of men…Well, God's sole usefulness would be to guarantee innocence…Don't wait for the Last Judgment. It takes place every day.[14]

In speaking of the Last Judgment, we derive, from what has come before, the eschatological nature of our ethical considerations. But we have found an eschatology that is situated in the transcendent relation brought about within the experience of the Other, seen on the face of the other with whom I uncover discourse. This eschatology breaks, at every instant, that thematization with which one objectifies another by creating a Judgment that is always yet to come; the divine judgment would stand beyond the totality.

Eschatology cannot mean the egoist protestation of a person, even for their own salvation, against history, or against the totality.[15] Instead, in eschatology, we find that, to quote, "The idea of infinity delivers the subjectivity from the judgment of history to declare it ready for judgment at every moment and…called to participate in this judgment, impossible without it."[16] We must consider what has been said regarding the open definition of "atheism." I suggest that "religion" and what is "religious" can be re-evaluated in a similar way and, in fact, this is already being done with remarkable consequences in support of the above considerations. The work of Rudolf Otto is notable for this re-evaluation of the "religious." As early as 1913 Otto describes religion as, "something that does not generally allow of definition, that needs to be experienced religiously. It is something that is experienced in a qualitative and specific religious moment, that is felt non-sensuously and exuberantly."[17] Levinas comments on the meaning of the religious, writing:

> This bond with the other which is not reducible to the representation of the other, but to his invocation, and in which invocation is not preceded by an understanding, I call *religion*... "Religion" remains the relationship to a being as a being.[18]

Taken with Otto, we can say that this relationship to a being as a being is the religious moment, as the moment of a curve is described by the relationship of the tangentials used in the calculation of the quadrature (returning to the calculus metaphor utilized in the Fourth Study). In this relation the full significance of the transcendent is revealed.

Though there may be a need for dialogue between my view of "religion" and the African view of "religion" intended by Hord and Lee, it is clear from the above that we share the notion of religion as a "fundamentally social expression of core philosophical ideas."[19] Here, the core philosophic conception of the idea of infinity breaks us from history and calls us as a participant in our own judgment, called fully into this participation when "fear of death is inverted into fear of committing murder."[20] Thus, this form of religion is hermeneutic in that it reopens the religious question of ethics at every encounter with the Other. This insistent reopening of the question is at once the postponement of the Last Judgment, the Judgment yet to come, while also being that Last Judgment that happens every day. Every day this question opens itself, indicating the judgment pending beyond history, not in some future historical event, for that would subsume the Judgment within the totality, but rather, beyond the grasp of history and overflowing the bounds of history while constituting the very possibility of history.

CONCLUSION

"I am because we are;" others constitute me in terms of otherness. I come to know myself through the Other, and this description denotes primarily the temporality of my being, my openness onto the world as unto the horizon. The transcendent is manifest in this relation, from the perspective of the precipice, between the horizon and myself. The phenomenology of the encounter on the precipice provided the backdrop for eschatological ethics at once atheistic and incorporative of the transcendent qua hermeneutics. The ontological I is self-reflective, and this always implies some critical approach that must remain skeptical, which is not the same as pessimistic.[21] In fact, the whole project of the current thesis has been to affirm a notion of the human being that can aspire to something great in the company of others again, that we might be again able to recognize great sages and saints among us and revere again the dignity and shame of being human in the world that offers no comfort except solidarity. It is this solidarity that serves as the basis of any faith. We do not hold hope and faith alone. We hold it *with* love or raise it up *against* tyranny and oppression. It is *for the widows and orphans* and it is *against the tyrant and oppressor*. The violence against the other has been indicted as violence against that Other which mediates my own being. And violence done against the other becomes violence against myself in a de-centralized, non-egoist sense belonging to self-regard and survival. This violence is recognized beyond myself, in the other whom I need, that needs me.

Camus goes on to say:

> At this limit "we are" paradoxically defines a new form of individualism. "We are" in terms of history, and history must reckon with "We are," which must in turn keep its place in history...Every collective action, every form of society, supposes a discipline, and the individual, without this discipline, is a stranger, bowed down under the weight of an inimical collectivity.[22]

Through the avenues opened by the above discussion, we have opened ourselves to others. We have found a way from the annihilation and alienation formerly attributed to "modern man." In this, we have chased the ghost of solidarity through the individualism of the twentieth century to arrive at the possibility of a new individuality. This emergent individualism is defined, it has been noted, by a superficial paradox in which "I am" only insofar as "We are." These two designators become inextricable from one another when the "I" is uncovered as being other-to-itself. "We are" and through this "we are," I retrieve myself from another. The we-subject is already designated by my assertion of the "I" because without the other alongside whom "I" form the "we" the "I" referent loses its sense. It is only from the "we" that the "I" can be drawn out, made distinct, pointed to, indicated, individuated. Yet, this individuality has to be uncovered; it remains concealed.

Like all worthwhile inquiries, ours has opened us to new possibilities. This work is a struggle against the opacity that formerly doomed us to alienation. Moving ahead, it would be a benefit to bring the "essence" of ἀλήθεια with us so as not to forget the work that all inquiry demands of us. There are no easy answers here, at the meridian of thought, were the zenith of one observer is the height of another.

Notes to the Concluding Study

[1] African proverb, formulated by John S. Mbiti, *African Religions and Philosophy*, 2nd ed. (Oxford: Heinemann, 1989), 141.

[2] Fred Lee Hord (Mzee Lasana Okpara) & Jonathan Scott Lee, "'I am because we are': An Introduction to Black Philosophy." *I Am Because We Are: Readings in Black Philosophy*, (Amherst, MA: University of Massachusetts Press, 1995), 11.

[3] Which translates: "At this limit, the 'We are' defines paradoxically a new individualism." The French from Albert Camus, *L'homme Révolte*, (Paris: Gallimard, 1951); 366—67.

[4] Asa G. Hillard III, Larry Williams, & Nia Damali, eds., *The Teachings of Ptahhotep: The Oldest Book in the World* (Atlanta: Blackwood Press, 1987); 16—37.

[5] A startling reference to "faces" here, given our concern with the work of Levinas. *The Book of the Dead: The Papyrus of Ani in the British Museum*, Egyptian text with interlinear transliteration, translation, introduction, and notes by E. A. Wallis Budge (London: Trustees of the British Museum, 1895), 348.

[6] Hord & Lee, "I am because we are…" 7.

[7] Ibid; 7—8.

[8] For more on the concept of generative themes, see Paulo Freiere *Pedagogy of the Oppressed*, trans. Myra Bergman Ramos, (New York: Continuum Press, 1970); 86—101.

[9] Joseph M. Nyasani, "The Ontological Significance of 'I' and 'We' in African Philosophy." *I, We and Body*, ed. Heinz Kimmerle, (Amsterdam: B. R. Grüner, 1989), 18.

[10] Ibid, 18.

[11] Ibid, 15.

[12] Russell, "A Free Man's Worship." *Why I Am Not a Christian: and other essays on religion and related subjects*, ed, Paul Edwards, (New York: George Allen & Unwin, 1957), 115.

[13] Jacques Derrida, *The Politics of Friendship*, trans. George Collins, (New York: Verso, 2005), 1. Derrida comments on the contradictory predicates of the sentence that: "Incompatible as they may appear and condemned to the oblivion of contradiction, here, in a sort of desperately dialectical desire, the two times already form two theses—two *moments*, perhaps—they concatenate, they appear *together*, they are summoned to appear, in the present: they present themselves as in a single stroke, in a single breath, in the same present, in the present itself. At the same time, and before who knows who, before who knows whose law. The *contretemps* looks favorably on the encounter, it responds without delay but without renunciation: no promised encounter without the possibility of a *contretemps*. As soon as there is more than one." I only intend to note Derrida's use of "breath" here and suggest again, as in the First Study, that the breath results as a culmination of a narrative of separation. This fissure arising at the origin disrupts a unity, which speaks qua being unified of difference already constituted. Finally, in the disruption, the idea of asymmetry constitutes the relation to the transcendent qua temporality—the transit through the Other on the detour toward being; being ontological.

[14] Albert Camus, *The Fall*, trans. Justin O'brien, (New York: Vintage International, 1991); 110—11.

[15] Levinas agrees. See, *Totality and Infinity*, 25.

[16] Ibid, 25.

[17] Rudolf Otto is a famous early example. See, for instance, "Buddhism and Christianity—Compared and Contrasted." Philip C. Almond trans. *Buddhist Christian Studies*, vol. 4 (1984); 87—101. In this article, originally given as a lecture by Otto in 1913 [Ibid, 3] religion is described as [Ibid, 89] We shall se what this "specific religious moment" might be in the work of Levinas.

[18] Levinas, "Is Ontology Fundamental?" *Entre Nous: Thinking-of-the-Other*, trans. Michael B. Smith & Barbara Harshav, (New York: Continuum Press, 2006), 7.

[19] Hord & Lee, "'I am because we are'…" 8.

[20] Levinas, *Totality and Infinity*, 244.

[21] In response to a question posed by H. Philipse, "Is the philosophical attitude—which is in essence a skeptical attitude—not in contradiction with the attitude of faith?" Levinas responded: "Skeptical" only means the fact of examining things, the fact of posing questions. I do not at all think that a question—or, at least, the original questioning—is only a deficiency of answers. Functional and even scientific questions—and many philosophical ones—await only answers. Questioning *qua* original attitude is a "relation" to that which no response can contain, to the "uncontainable"; it becomes responsibility. Every response contains a "beside the point" and appeals to an un-said [*dé-dit*]. For the full dialogue, see Emmanuel Levinas, "Questions and Answers." Bettina Bergo trans. *Of God Who Comes to Mind*, (Stanford: Stanford University Press, 1998); 79—99.

[22] Albert Camus, *The Rebel*, Anthony Bower trans. (New York: Vintage International, 1991), 297.

INTERLUDE[1]

1. What did Nietzsche do? This is not philosophy or philology or one of the many other studies of mankind's loves It was the love of the self that Nietzsche was concerned with and he hated those systems that confounded the self and rendered it impotent. He stood by the way tugging the carpet from under the lofty marble of Schopenhauer and Wagner until the effigies he had built of them toppled from their pedestals in a symbolic public gesture.

2. And how am I to fill this space? It is an intimidating prospect. Like the future, one that I can almost see but never bares fruit until I strike the keys. So this is creation. No, because now the words are static and something is lost.

3. Am I doing this in praise of Nietzsche? Is imitation flattery or is this sarcasm, or is it a matter of perspective. In a sense, would not my own perspective hold more weight? But I am not writing this for me, I am writing it as a study, as a study on Nietzsche the writer who promised it would not be easy. Am I idolizing Nietzsche? It is comforting to be reminded that inherent in the concept of an idol is an essential falsehood.

4. Perhaps it would be best to discuss the *Untimely Meditations* in a more measured and levelheaded manner. After all, it is serious academic consideration that they deserve. Their importance is, in part, due to the extremely personal nature of the writing and the choice of themes presented in them. Opening with a treatment of Strauss reflects the deep resentment of popular opinion Nietzsche held at the time of this meditation. Philistinism is the overt accusation made against the Germans of his day. In this rejection of accepted cultural wisdom, Nietzsche begins to sow a deep seeded individualism that encourages everyone to seek their own way and test their own truths. But there is also an inevitable isolation, a cutting off between the 'me' and the 'they.' Left to himself, a growing rift between he and his friends (particularly the Wagner's) Nietzsche is alone with himself and reflecting in that context. And so results a very personal expression in which we learn philosophy is inseparable from the philosopher.

5. When I was 13, I stole a Nietzsche collection from the public library. It is now one of the only remaining artifacts of my adolescence.

6. In this context we can begin to see a narrative build of Nietzsche's life and his philosophy. Narrative is important to an overall understanding of Nietzsche's thought and the emphasis he sometimes put on myth. Myths are essentially narratives and the kind of symbolic narrative Nietzsche was so keen on dissecting in his project of revaluation. His view of history in 'On the uses and advantages of history for life' implies certain narrative structures. But those structures are not self-contained. Are we really to become walking encyclopedias gorged on cultural happenings? What does this imply about our freedom or creativity? Perhaps Nietzsche is manifesting a rejection of Schopenhauer's escape into experiences of artistic creativity. There arises elbowroom for a new kind of creativity that is not an escape but an affirmation of that which creates.

7. I will now quote Gabriel Garcia Marquez: "Many years later, as he faced the firing squad, Colonel Aureliano Buendia was to remember that distant afternoon when his father took him to discover ice." The wonderful opening line of *One Hundred Years of Solitude*. And one hundred more to discover what use this is to me. Perhaps I am reminded that Marquez won the Nobel Prize, and so

he did. What use is the Nobel to me except to recall that Sartre refused it? And now that we come to Sartre, again, what does this mean for our freedom. For now we are thinking of freedom because I quote Marquez. But even he is just a part of the common history that we share and partake in. To us, just part of the story we tell that is our culture and his books are an avenue through which one can become "cultured."

8. And now, Titus Andronicus!
    "Why, tis no matter; if no tribune hears me speak,
    They would not mark me, or if they did mark,
    They would not pity me, yet plead I must;
    Therefore I tell my sorrows to the stones;
    Who, though they cannot answer my distress,
    Yet in some sort they are better than the tribunes,
    For that they will not intercept my tale:
    When I do weep, they humbly at my feet
    Receive my tears and seem to weep with me;
    And, were they but attired in grave weeds,
    Rome could afford no tribune like to these.
    A stone is soft as wax,—tribunes more hard than stones; A stone is silent, and offendeth not,
    And tribunes with their tongues doom men to death."

9. "Therefore I tell my sorrow to the stones;" here again we find twofold solace in the history by which we become specialists. Shakespeare recants the tragedies of the

Romans. Nietzsche rebuking Strauss, Schopenhauer, awkwardly praising Wagner so that the stiltedness of his words betrays his disapproval.

10. Better then to tell your sorrow to the stones of history than to tell them to the tribunal who dooms men to death. What can history judge in which it has not itself been judged already? If we weep then history, like the stones, receives our tears and seems to weep with us as we retell it with so much wailing and beating of our breasts.

11. I hope I have helped, contributed in some way to the understanding of the *Untimely Meditations*, to Nietzsche's project. I hope I have raised some questions. I hope you'll accept my apologies. The text has evoked these thoughts in me but I take responsibility for them.

12. Most of all, I hope I have been bold and offensive to Reason.

DIGRESSION

Now, I feel obliged to address my own purposes. "Herewith I have completed my confession of faith. It is the confession of an individual; and what can such an individual do against all the world, even when his voice is audible everywhere!" With these words the essay "David Strauss, the confessor and the writer" is concluded. I think I share with Nietzsche, above all things to share with him, a need for this type of confession but too often Nietzsche's confession takes the form of a negation.

The accusation of philistinism in this essay seems to ignore the fact that it is the selfsame philistinism that informs Nietzsche's thought as well as the common persons, for is Nietzsche himself not a German? He is, in a very full sense because he is aware of himself as a German and of the Germany into which he has grown. This does not mean he should not be critical, in fact there is all the more reason for him to be critical since only German's can determine the ultimate course of Germany. I mean this in a literal sense, for even if the German's are to be conquered from every side it is still the German's that must bear that defeat and respond in the German way to their demise. And then who could be more fully German? But I digress.

Noam Chomsky has commented that it is the job of the citizenry and of the press, the intelligencia, of a country to criticize that country's policies because they have the power to affect change. The US media criticizing the Russian government is easy because there is no threat. What the US media should be doing is criticizing the US government because that is where they can make meaningful progress. Nietzsche seems to share in this thinking to an extent and this fuels his criticisms of Strauss.

He claims Strauss' moral imperative is reducible to "Live like a man and not as an ape or a seal!" The imperative is useless because under the concept of 'man' falls such a huge variety of phenomena. Here is a bridge to the next meditation, "On the uses and disadvantages of history for life." Ultimately, Strauss provides an explanation of historical circumstances that offers an apology for philistinism. This ideology has been widely adapted, claims Nietzsche.

Strauss, like Hegel, offers a static historical interpretation. The advantage of Nietzsche, and here I play confessor, lies in its dynamism. This is the parallel I want to draw out by quoting Marquez. Indeed, from the lines of Shakespeare arise a historical dynamism that points out the importance of interpretation at once with that of self-determination. It is interesting to note that V. I. Lenin coined the phrase 'self-determination.' For one, it affects how we interpret self-determination. But, more important to our purposes here, is the fact that Lenin, writing in a Marxist tradition, intends self-determination to be a concept regarding historic-political development: a creative development toward something new. Nietzsche pushes for this same creative energy and does so emphatically. His force derives simultaneously from the profundity of his arguments and the persuasion of his rhetoric. The Bolsheviks fell prey to the same moment of crystallization that Hegelianism doomed itself to. The USSR was forever defying the future happiness it promised in a blind reverence for a militant revolutionary present that was idolized. As I've said, there is something false inherent in the concept of an idol.

So it would be false of me, and a discredit, to have written my meditation in idolization of Nietzsche. But I can't help feeling a creative element in philosophy that is too often neglected in the contemporary tradition. So, rightfully, I responded in affirmation of myself, of my own interests, and out of a longstanding solidarity I feel with Nietzsche that has very little to do with scholarly pursuits.

Notes to the Interlude

[1] This interlude is a meditation on Nietzsche's *Untimely Meditations*, trans. R. J. Hollingdale, (Cambridge: Cambridge University Press, 1997). As it is a meditation, and an exercise in free writing, this shall be the extent of the article's citation.

ON THE FREEDOM OF ACTION

Prolegomena

As I learned to philosophize, I came across many striking and curiously written artifacts that stirred me to seek the truth for myself. The inspiration provided by the text is but the beginning of philosophy proper—which is not the same as the study of philosophy. To study philosophy is to learn the written works of dead or dying men and women. To philosophize oneself is something altogether different.

The study of philosophy is then a kind of preparatory work, a prolegomena to philosophy proper where one formulates the thoughts themselves beyond the confines of historical texts. The first part of this essay is such a prolegomena and it concerns the work of Roderick Chisholm, whose words inspired my own thinking on the subject of freedom and responsibility.

Though inspiration is not outright agreement, it does call one to the truth, and so something truthful must be identified even if the full consequences of an argument's conclusion must be rejected in the end.

So let us limit ourselves, for purely practical purposes, to an article written by Chisholm and read by me in a formative stage of my philosophical development. The critique of the essay "Human Freedom and the Self,"[1] serves as a prolegomena to the arguments of the current work.

Chisholm beings "Human Freedom and the Self" with a reference to Aristotle. We are directed to *Physics*, where Aristotle writes, "A staff moves, and is moved by a hand, which is moved by a man,"[2] It thus appears that human agents, under an Aristotelian assumption, can constitute the primary cause of a given chain of events. It is this conception of the Self that Chisholm is interested in, the concept of Self as an agent capable of being a prime mover. He goes on to argue for a re-evaluation of Free Will—claiming that the perennial debate concerning the nature of Free Will has been cast in terms that render responsible human agency incoherent within both deterministic and indeteriministic views of human action. In fact, Chisholm is hesitant to use the noun "Free Will" at all, as he agrees with Locke, that it is not a question of *"whether the will be free"*; it is the question of *"whether a man be free"*[3]—is the agent free to do those things she does in fact will or not. The question of the freedom of the will is therefore inappropriate. The manner in which Chisholm argues for these conclusions, and the support he provides for his arguments, will be considered in more detail. This prolegomena concludes with a refutation aimed at the Aristotelian ontological model used by Chisholm in the construction of his concept of "agency." That the argument lacks a coherent model for the agent that it intends to be a prime mover undermines its claim that the agent is capable of being an undetermined origin of determined events, although Chisholm is to be commended for his intuitive rejection of the traditional determinist framework.

Chisholm's understanding of determinism and indeterminism are vital to his arguments and are expressed by him as follows: the determinist view is that in which every event involved in an act is caused by some other event, and the indeterminist view is that in which the act, or some event essential to the act, is not caused at all. The problem Chisholm identifies with each view is that they are both incompatible with the conception of a responsible human agent. If a person is to be responsible, then what was to happen has to be entirely necessitated by the person who is the cause of what was to happen. If we accept the determinist view, then the agent is not responsible because every event was causally determined beforehand by the immediately preceding event and so on ad infinitum, thus no event was determined by any person who was not himself determined by past events. If, on the other hand, we accept the indeterminist view, then a person cannot be responsible simply because an event that is not determined is an event without a cause. Therefore, no event that is not determined can have as its cause a responsible agent—such an event has no cause at all. It does not matter whether events are caused externally by states of affairs, or internally by a person acting on beliefs, desires etc. the world still ends up a deterministic world under the indeterminist's view because all events, states of affairs, or what have you are caused by other events or states of affairs.

Chisholm offers a standard stratagem against determinism, namely the claims of compatibilist philosophers[4], and shows why this stratagem is unsuccessful. The stratagem states that the claim a) "he could have done otherwise" is logically equivalent to the claim b) "if he had chosen to do otherwise, then he would have done otherwise." The object of this stratagem is to show that both determinism and divine providence are compatible with human responsibility. Both determinism and divine providence allow for claim (b) to be true because even if all of a person's actions are causally necessitated, a person could still be such that *if* they had chosen to do other than they did, then they would have *in fact* done other than they did. If this follows and (b) is consistent with determinism, then (a), as equivalent to (b), is also consistent with determinism. Moral responsibility and the determinist view are thus compatible.

However, the above stratagem fails, according to Chisholm. The problem lies in the equivocation of (a) to (b). It could be the case that statement (b) is true, while statement (a) is false. The claim that "a person could have done otherwise" cannot be equivalent to the claim that "if a person had chosen to do otherwise, then they would have done otherwise" unless it also obtains that (c) "a person could have chosen to do otherwise"; i.e., that it was possible for a person to have chosen other than they did. Statement (c) is rejected because a person could be such that if they had chosen to do otherwise, then they would have done otherwise, and yet it is also the case that it is not possible that they could have chosen otherwise. Therefore, (b) could be accepted, and yet (a) cannot. The key to Chisholm's success is in his recognition of the inability of the compatibilist to produce a model of agency in which the agent himself is more than a determined part of events unfolding across time. This realization motivates him to shift focus and reexamine some of the basic assumption of the Free Will debate. He asks whether or not there might be a conception of action that is neither deterministic nor indeterministic?

On such a view it would be the case that not every event involved in an act is caused by another event and yet the act is not something that is not caused at all, leaving open the possibility that at least one event involved in the act is caused by something other than another event, namely the act is caused by the agent. It is here that my reservations regarding Chisholm's conclusions arise, though we must hear him unreservedly through to his finish. I am fully endorsing Chisholm's version of Locke's concern, yet I am without support for the Aristotelian ontology implicit in Chisholm's arguments. For the moment, let us remain focused on "Human Freedom and the Self" and the distinction drawn between two types of causation therein.

Borrowing terms from medieval philosophy, the distinction is made between two kinds of causation and this distinction is viewed to be indispensable to understanding the nature of human responsibility. Using this distinction, we need not commit to the statement "there was some event involved in the act that was not caused." Transeunt Causation is that in which one event or state of affairs caused another event or state of affairs, whereas Immanent

Causation is that in which an agent, as distinguished from an event, causes an event or states of affairs. Causation becomes altogether different if events are not caused only by other events. The provided example is of a cerebral event, the motive to raise a hand, being Immanently Caused. All of the skeletal-muscular movements involved in the execution of the act of raising the hand are caused Transeuntly. There are objections to this distinction, and Chisholm addresses the two he sees as most threatening.

The first objection rests on three premises. If a person does anything in the example of raising a hand then what they do is just raise their hand; they do not do anything to their brain and it is given as possible that they may not even know that they have a brain. If the person did not do anything to their brain, then the raising of their hand was caused by some event within the brain. The distinction between Transeunt and Immanent Causation is erased as everything involved in an action turns out to be no more than a relation of events of states of affairs. A strong objection, and Chisholm responds rather succinctly, though he admits it is the easier of the two objects for him to answer. He cites the distinction made by A. I. Melden between "making something happen" and "doing something"; that is, "between making an event (A) happen" and "doing something (A)."[5] In this sense "doing something A" is the result of an intentional act. When a person is said to be "making something A happen" they are said to be causing events to happen in conjunction with their intentional act, and that these conjunctional events are not in themselves intentional acts and may be events of which the acting parties have no awareness whatsoever. Even though a person may not do something intentional to or with the brain itself, it does not follow from this that she is not the Immanent Cause of some event within her brain—and though she may be unaware of this brain event, she is, nevertheless, the cause of said brain event.

Chisholm only briefly lights upon the concept of "intention" in his discussion of Melden's distinctions. He fails to pursue the subject any further as he develops his essay. This omission, or the negligent treatment of intentionality as an issue of importance greatly affects the eventual outcome of his reasoning. I will show how Chisholm's refutation of the second objection reveals that the relevance of intentionality to his overall project was not sufficiently treated. The refutation to the second objection offered by Chisholm fails, whereas a refutation of the same objection would succeed if the refutation were based on defining the role of intentionality in the performance of an action.

The second refutation is considered to be the more difficult of the two. It claims that if event A were not caused by any other event or state of affairs but was caused by an agent, then the agent could not have undergone a change or produced an event that in turn caused A to happen. If the agent did not undergo change or produce an event that caused event A to happen, of what then did the agent's causation consist? There would be no difference between an agent having caused event A to happen and event A's just happening. The response to this objection is that the claim of a difference between a person causing A to happen and A just happening was already justified in the rebuttal of the first objection, considered above. In this case, event A is caused, as opposed to having no cause, and it is a person who causes event A.

If the event A just happened, there would be no cause for A happening. In Chisholm's scenario, there is a brain event A, the agent caused A to happen but there was nothing done to cause A. By this account the agent undergoes no change, nor does the agent produce any event that in turn causes the events of the agent's action. The question "in what does the agent's causation consist?" reappears. How can the agent be said to be the cause of any event? We shall return to this issue.

For now, let us focus on Chisholm's assertion that it is plausible that the notion of Immanent Cause is clearer than is the notion of Transeunt Cause. Only by understanding the causal efficacy of the agent, of the Self, that the concept of causation is comprehensible at all.[6] Locke is invoked. The question of Free Will, qua Locke, is inappropriate. If there is indeed a faculty of the will, the question is not "is the will free?" but "is the person free to act in accordance with their will or not to act?" We are to suppose that the answer to these questions will not reveal anything about moral responsibility. There is a distinction between *actus imperatus* and *actus elicitus*. Chisholm explains the difference is that *actus imperatus* is the freedom to do whatever it is that a person wills or sets out to do, whereas *actus elicitus* is the freedom to will or to set out to do the things that a person will do or set out to do—a nuanced difference, one that requires careful handling. Responsibility seems to call for a version of the prime-mover-unmoved. Nothing can cause the agent, which in turn causes the event to happen. Chisholm calls this special case of causation Agent Causation.

There is a bit more to Chisholm's essay remaining. The above consists of an exegesis of the main points made therein. Before we consider Chisholm's concluding remarks, permit a critique of the work thus far. It is not entirely clear of what the agent's causation consists. What work is the agent doing? In order to be responsible the agent has to do some work with her general condition. A certain context is presented to the subject, he understands the context and so on, and he makes decisions regarding how to act on the various given situation in which he lives. Though Immanent Cause is promoted as a clear and distinct category, its horizon is not yet determined. Is immanent cause the binary operation of the will as it "does something A" and "makes something A happen"? Immanent cause has thus a double-edged internal mechanism. Is this why Locke is used to support the supposition that Transeunt causation was apparent in the world of *inanimate objects*? But even such a supposition would not circumvent the objection that there is no significant difference between "doing something A" and "making something happen A" if the only admissible cause of all events or states of affairs is other events and states of affairs (whether in the brain or elsewhere) and the consequences of this chain of events is just an infinite progress of events. This is determinism on Chisholm's own terms. What is the agent that is acting in the world? The answer to this question does not come easy to Chisholm's pen. The subject is skirted. It is unmoved in exact proportion to that which it moves. But what reaches beyond its own sublime tranquility to stir the world of action?

Two unfounded conceptions underscore all of the above distinctions. One is the *specific way* in which Chisholm has opposed determinism to indeterminism. It is important that determinism is defined first and supposes that, "every event that is involved in an act is cause by some other event." So events cause events, and certain discrete series of events can be called acts. Acts are performed. Therefore, there must be some performer of the act. But indeterminism is in the odd position of being opposed to the view that the act, or some event essential to the act, is not caused. Therefore any conception of the agent from the indeterminist view must concede that it is possible for events to have no cause. Thus the will does not "cause itself" because the will, if conceptualized as an event itself (e.g. the making of the decision to act, deciding on a particular course of action when the circumstances provide for a manifold of possible courses of action) would, upon only minor reflection, permit the formation of several potential hypotheses regarding what the consequences of any given course of action might be. The very conditionality of determinism lies in *the possibility of the agent to conceive of causation as a concept upon which she can act*. The intentionality of consciousness does not remove her from the causal chain, for the objects of intention are given to the subject by the mere fact of her existence—the room just appears as it is, even when I populate it with familiar artifacts, which I've happened to come across over the years. The room is still naked, I am confronted each time I reason with the judge and jury of experience to justify my judgment. The agent has the ability to identify causation in the world and this cognitive ability contributes to its actions as well as to the will to act.

Chisholm's argument thus far has bifurcated each time the agent is approached, as if he eludes identifying the subject, of violating it with hypothesis. The best evasive efforts amount to fill conceptual space between events with causes and events without causes, which could amount to a synthesis if only the unity of the oppositions lent name to the third concept, the stumbling Agent Causation. But no unity presents and only further bifurcation, multiplied dualism. In between polarities the agent hides. Unmoving. Moving.

The agent must do work even if determinism holds. But if determinism is maintained the agent of Agent Causation is stranded in indeterminism, powerless less it is swept up in the causal chain, the act it perpetuates upon the causal chain contributing to the events that form the conditions of future life for the agent. It is as if, metaphorically speaking, the agent is alone in a very small room. From this room, the agent reaches out and makes changes in the world, but remains immune to movement from the exterior world, which determines it very little, if at all. Chisholm seems to have painted himself into the corner of this room. Did he account for a way out? Has he waited? How is it that the agent does anything? How does she reach from her room? Or is it a window?

What is necessary is to show *how it is that the agent operated freely in a determined world.* When Chisholm was active, the pursuit of this necessity would have been called a compatibilist pursuit—but the need I intend is merely the *possibility of the conception of "should have done otherwise."* How is it possible to even say, "so and so ought to have done different than they did." This act implies judgment, another in a series of acts, implicit once the schema of "will" is deployed. To will has always been the transition between thought and action, when the agent intends to do something and then that thing is done. The will always implies time.

I have suggested that intentionality is the key component of agency neglected by the account presented in "Human Freedom and the Self." I had compared Chisholm's agent to a person in a room. A small room. Intentionality is not always in a room. It is sometimes outside, in a city, walking down the street, riding in a car or on the subway. Different situations inform the intentionality of the subject, giving the agent the tools to operate on the manifold of experience. The agent, the very possibility of her ability to act being rooted in a given world with certain determined qualities without these determined conditionals providing her the context within which to perform the act, would never have the opportunity to make the free choice to act. The intention to act moves the will to the actualization of what thought deemed possible. Responsibility comes with success or failure in the execution of a possibility that had been decided upon. We decide "I should do this," and the act is done, only the judgment of failure makes sense of the thought "he ought to have done otherwise." To "should have done otherwise" is the judgment of consequence, events have led to a state of affairs that should be other than they are. To what extent is the agent a victim of these events?

The variety of description enumerated by Chisholm, all reflecting the ways in which events are caused become practical, are not presented as explanation, but as a phenomenological description of the kinds of events in which we find agents engaged with the world of experience. Locke can come to the fore. It is unimportant whether or not the Will is a "free" Will. The word "free" adds nothing to the concept of Will that is not already assumed in the postulation of the very possibility of the Will. The Will *acts*, and it acts of its own accord qua *self-determination*. Is it free of causation? No. It is the agent that causes the will, in the sense that the Will is a product of the concert of the agent's physiological means of action. The Will is the end of these means because it is the actualization of the agent's ability to move from the idea to the act—to execute the idea in the world.

Some physiological factors may be superfluous to self-consciousness, or to the Will, indeed to many factors that constitute the being of the agent. They are superfluous when, supposing them absent from the agent, either at birth as a consequence of events in the agent's life, the agent does not then cease to be a self-conscious agent with intentionality. Consider for a moment how that intentionality might change, how the affection of this intentionality could be effected by a change in the physiological constitution of the being.

Take, for instance, a person who was born with functionality in both legs, but as the result of an accident, she loses the use of both legs. The agent is then positioned to realign her intentionality toward the world and toward herself. How does she do this? Through processes both creative and free. This example is a useful one because we are quick to interpret the loss of one's upright mobility as confining, as a sentence to a kind of imprisonment in a chair or some other literal crutch. But in transition from one who walks upright to one who does not, the agent must make decisions about how to meet the challenge her condition puts before her. The agent may not have determined that such an accident occurs in her life (though we could easily imagine a scenario where the agent does determine it, either through fault or intentional self-harm). Regardless, the agent can and does determine the intentional stance toward her circumstances and develops her own idiosyncratic methods of coping and rehabilitation. Taking into consideration personal history, upbringing, circumstances regarding the accident, subsequent circumstances, and possible futures the agent may come to inhabit, the agent can begin to formulate a new intentional stance. A strict determinist would argue that the agent has no freedom in this conception, that in fact all those things that go into the agent's intentional decision are externally determined and thus determined the agent's decision. But here, again, the agent is made too small. It is forgotten that the agent *is* by necessity some of those factors which the determinist is determined to label "external" and thus dissociate from the agent's basic constitution.

The history of the agent belongs to the agent. It is his own history and constitutes him. The agent is spread over time.[7] However, the agent cannot be "composed" of temporality simply because time does not appear as an object. Thus the Will is not an object within the chain of causal events, e.g. as a billiard ball is an object in the chain of causation whose consequence is a combination shot in a corner pocket. The body is the interface of the Will with the world at any given time. If we accept that Chisholm utilizes an Aristotelian ontology, then we can define where his argument fails. Under such a framework, the agent cannot be dynamic, he cannot be his past—he must be a thing that persists over time but cannot be composed by temporality.

Temporality cannot effect the agent; nothing can be permitted to effect the agent without rendering the agent unfree. But with the development of a more rigorously expanded agent, allow him the dynamism and elasticity of time, give to him his temporality (as, experientially, temporality is given to the agent) and, though a certain, absolute freedom is lost, the only freedom that matters is redeemed—the freedom to act or not to act in accordance with the Will.

The ideal, absolute freedom that would remind us of Sartre is refuted. Chisholm seems to demand this kind of unattached freedom of the agent; the agent must be either unmoved or unfree. But, practically, the freedom that Chisholm cares about is preserved. Locke is vindicated. Though initial criticism is sure to be met, any critic must be careful to follow the thread of reason through the necessary relationship of freedom and determinism or else they will miss the point—for Chisholm's Aristotelian ontology is not the ontology of Aristotle. It is a professor of philosophy using Aristotle as a means to his end, as most writers of philosophy are wont to do with those who wrote before them.

Let us return to exegesis. The remainder of Chisholm's article is admirable for its help in further elucidating what I mean by a "larger agent." If the tiny agent in her room is abandoned, or better, freed from her conceptual bondage, then she is free to enter into the various relations that constitute the modality of her being in the world. The agent has simple components, such as a Will unburdened of the question of its freedom, but the agent herself is a complex creature—perhaps complex beyond full expression. The tiny agent could do no work. The agent posited in the current essay does meaningful work that results in causal consequences arising from her intentionality. How does the conclusion of "Human Freedom and the Self" contribute to this understanding, since the article is, itself, not supportive of such a conception of the self?

A complex agent with a simple Will is a nexus of causal relations. Innumerable causes feed into the processes constitutive of the agent. Due to the extremity of causal forces exerting themselves on the agent's body, no definitive cause is determinative of the agent's actions in the world. Thus the agent is indetermined, not because she has no cause, but because she has such an overabundance of causes that no one cause, or even set of causes, necessitates the agent's behaving in one way or another. The work the agent does is in her decision regarding *which set of cause or causes she will act on and in what way she will act on those causes that are presented to her.* The decision consists of the agent's intentionality toward a project outlined for herself and toward which she works with intent. The project could be simple (raising a hand) or more complex (applying to college, or learning how to live without the use of one's legs). A project may change, or be carried out for an indetermined length of time, that is, until the agent has completed the project or abandoned it in favor of another. It is at the agent's discretion that a project is complete, to be returned to or revivified.

Chisholm claims that there is no "science of man." His final distinction is between a Hobbist and a Kantian approach to an agent's decision-making ability. The Hobbist approach says, "If all the variables are known, all of a person's beliefs, desires, etc, then their behavior can be accurately predicted." This is akin to knowing precisely which causal factors necessitate a person's actions. The Kantian approach denies the logical connection between wanting and doing, refuting the causal connection as well. The analysis carried out in the current essay has adapted the Kantian approach. Because the number of causal factors is so vast no science of man is possible and no logical or causal connection is enough to necessitate the agent's course of action. Leibniz can thereby be justified in his claim that a desire or motive might "incline without necessitating."[8] Chisholm further explores this possibility by analyzing a scenario in which a judge can resist initiating a bribe, but cannot resist a bribe once he knows that it is available. This consideration is not particularly useful here, and it does little to substantiate the claims made regarding Agent Causation.

What is missing from Agent Causation is not freedom, but the Self. The theory cannot account for a viable agent that does work within a causal chain. The agent presented by the theory is so small as to be non-existent. Expand the agent, abandon Chisholm's Aristotelian ontology in favor of a more phenomenological one, reconsider the consequences of determinism, and what emerges is something more coherent and realistic than a Mover Unmoved. There is even room for moral responsibility, as we shall see. Determinism can no longer be blamed if determinism is insufficient to necessitate the agent's actions. Through an intentional relation with its own causal factors, the agent is capable of self-determination.

We now turn away from the work of this prolegomena to the argument proper, which will greatly expand upon the foundational work of defining responsible agency that was undertaking in the prolegomena's preliminary critique.

Notes to the Prolegomena

[1] I encountered this article in Chisholm, "Human Freedom and the Self." *Agency and Responsibility*, ed. Laura Waddell Ekstrom, (Boulder, CO: Westview Press, 2001); 126—137. All subsequent references to Chisholm's essay refer to this edition.

[2] Aristotle, "Physics." *The Complete Works of Aristotle: The Revised Oxford Translations Vol. 1*, ed. Jonathan Barnes, (Princeton: Princeton University Press, 1995), 427. Chisholm identifies the Bekker marginal pagination, locating the quote at 256^a. The full relevant passage, in slightly different translation, runs from lines 6 to 10 and reads, "Further, in the latter case [when an object is set in motion, not because of something else which moves the mover, but by the mover itself] either the mover immediately precedes the last thing in the [causal] series, or there may be one or more intermediate links: e.g. the stick moves the stone and is moved by the hand, which again is moved by the man; in the man, however, we have reached a mover that is not so in virtue of being moved by something else." The general conclusion reached by Aristotle through this line of argumentation can be found in the *Physics* at 258^b4—9: "From what has been said, then, it is evident that that which primarily imparts motion is unmoved for, whether that which is in motion but moved by something leads straight to the first unmoved, or whether it leads to what is in motion but moves itself and stops its own motion, on both suppositions we have the result that in all cases of things being in motion that which primarily imparts motion is unmoved."

[3] Locke, *Essay Concerning Human Understanding*, bk. ii, ch. 21.

[4] Chisholm directs us to Jonathan Edwards, *Freedom of the Will*, (New Havens, 1957) and G. E. Moore, *Ethics*, ch.6, (Home University Library, 1912) as paradigms of Compatibilism.

[5] An elaboration of this distinction may be found in A. I. Melden, *Free Action*, (London, 1961). Chisholm indicates ch. 3 as significant, noting that Melden's ultimate conclusions differ dramatically from Chisholm's view.

[6] I pause here to note that the argument put forth in "Human Freedom and the Self" could be greatly augmented and improved upon by a more thorough reading of Kant.

[7] These insights result from a personal conversation with Dr. Matthew Pierlott occurring in the fall of 2007. This theme recurred with frequency in our discussions until the summer of 2009. In general, the work of Martin Heidegger is also of use to understanding my arguments here, and I acknowledge this influence without requiring a particular passage to illuminate the insights provided in the current essay.

[8] In a 1707 letter to Coste: Leibniz, "Lettre a Mr. Coste de la Nécessité et de la Contingence." *Opera Philosophica*, ed. Erdmann, 447—9.

On the Possibility of Responsible Freedom

Each man lives for himself, uses his freedom to achieve his personal goals and feels in his whole being that right now he can or cannot do such-and-such an action; but as soon as he does it, this action, committed at a certain moment in time becomes irreversible and makes itself the property of history, in which it has not a free but predetermined significance.[1]

ON THE CONCEPT OF RESPONSIBLE FREEDOM

To summarize the preceding prolegomena, the question of determinism's relation to freedom and moral responsibility finds resolution in a sound theory of personal identity. The Free Will debate has, by and large, been dominated by a discussion concerning the nature of determinism and its relevance to moral responsibility. If determinism, being the view that every event is necessarily caused by some previous event, is a fact, then there appears to be little room for praise or blame where a person's actions are concerned. This is a simplified expression of the general stance held by those philosophers called "incompatibilists," those maintaining that moral responsibility is incompatible with determinism. The thesis of the current essay takes determinism to be of importance while denying the incompatibility of determinism with freedom and responsibility. The theory to be explored reveals determinism to be inconsequential to freedom and necessary to moral responsibility. A sound model of the Self shows determinism to be non-lethal to freedom while the epistemological elements of an agent's decision-making processes recommends the centrality of determinism in a functional theory of moral responsibility. At one time, the stance taken in this essay would have been labeled a "compatibilist" theory because freedom, determinism, and responsibility co-exist. But it is not compatibilist in the traditional sense, because determinism is taken to have no bearing on an individual's freedom. The interrelationship of the three concepts named above will be dealt with in greater detail as we progress toward a reasonable model of agency in the human person, in the Self. Agent Causation was a commendable theory for its focus on the nature of the agent, thought it fails to adequately defend the God-like powers it bestows upon the agent as a mover unmoved.[2]

The theory of Agent Causation discussed in the prolegomena gives us the insight that the question of whether or not an agent was free to do what it wills to do would not prove whether or not the agent is responsible for its actual actions.[3] Certainly, though Chisholm's theory makes "somewhat far-reaching assumptions about the self or the agent,"[4] his theory is correct to focus on the formulation of the agent.

Two fundamental concepts are central to reconciling the metaphysics of freedom to moral responsibility. One is a theory of Self or agency; that is, a theory that explains how the agent is constituted as an entity in the world. This definition of the Self ties directly to the second fundamental: an ontology that resolves the rift between compatibilist and incompatibilist theories by showing that determinism is not deadly to the agent's freedom and is, in fact, conducive to her responsibility. A full theory of personal identity would better articulate the full ramifications of these fundamental concepts—however, such a complete view is not permitted by the scope of this essay.[5] The purpose of our current work is to focus on those fundamental issues involved in the metaphysics[6] of freedom. A brief, coherent model of agency will be forwarded using onto-epistemological arguments from a phenomenological perspective. It will be shown, using this model of the Self, of the agent, that determinism is reconciled with freedom and responsibility.

MODEL OF THE SELF

Having already dissociated the current theory from the theory of Agent Causation, this essay must answer the concession that a formulation of the self is of central importance to the question of whether of not the agent is free *and* responsible in his actions. How is such a Self to be conceptualized? Might the existence of the agent entail freedom and responsibility in his very functionality? Keep in mind the distinction between the Hobbist and the Kantian views on the relationship between what the agent wants/desires on one hand and what the agent actually does. The Hobbist sees the relationship as simple; the Kantian sees it as complex. A science of man is possible with the Hobbist; it is not possible for the Kantian. It is the Kantian approach that will be adapted here.

The Kantian approach, with minor alterations, can be defended in two ways. The first appeals to the role of subjectivity in an explanation of agency. What we seek is a definition of the Self. To ask "what is the Self?" is to inquire what it is that constitutes the inquirer. Inquiry proceeds from a certain perspective that is always somebody's subjective perspective and, in this instance, directs her intention toward explaining that very subjectivity which she herself *is*. There opens the barest hermeneutics. An inquiry being made into the nature of the Self, which is the very entity that is herself the inquirer, is hermeneutic because there are implicit intuitions regarding the Self that the inquiry follows. For instance, the Self *is* an inquirer; she can be said to cognize. Further, she is an entity that can be conceived as inquiring into herself, and it is therefore assumed to be self-aware, or self-conscious. Consciousness itself has already been assumed in the admission of cognition. That said, consciousness is necessarily always "consciousness of…"—there must be something other than consciousness that consciousness is conscious of.[7] The problems associated with subjectivity are perennial problems because all of our knowledge is acquired through subjective means. This is not the same as saying "all knowledge is subjective," for, after Husserl, we must acknowledge that the latter statement does not quite mean what we have taken it to mean. Any valid claim that "there is no objective knowledge," or that "all knowledge is subjective" is equivalent to "all knowledge as a conscious phenomenon is subject to the laws of human consciousness: the so-called forms and laws of knowledge are merely functional form of consciousness, or laws governing such functional forms, i.e. psychological laws."[8] Epistemological limits support the Kantian approach. These epistemic concerns have served a dual purpose, for through them is begun the process of building the agent from its foundational subjectivity. It is appropriate to address the relation of this agent to some concepts of causality.

Before moving forward it should be made clear that the discussion of the agent up to this point has included no mention of the agent's cause. Although there has been successful description of what an agent is. The point is made explicit only to indicate the possibility that the causal connections composing individual subjects do not necessarily determine the subject. Such a possibility will be taken up as we proceed.

At this time, consider the second argument in favor of the Kantian approach. In this view we discover the relevance of determinism to the model of self, and thereby to freedom as well. Formerly, I had accused Chisholm of making his agent "too small."[9] My accusation derives from an argument made by Daniel Dennett regarding formulations of agency popular in the Free Will debate. Essentially Dennett claims that if everything is externalized by making the subject very small, then the subject is reduced almost to a conceptual point that has no surface area with which it may interact with anything.[10] Dennett, like myself, considered the question "could the agent have done other than he did?" Such a question is a matter of interpretation. In interpreting, a person does not simply create a signification for some bare thing that it encounters in the world, rather, the thing is already involved in certain significations that are entailed in the person's understanding of the world and so interpretation merely functions to make those signification clear to consciousness. Dennett claims, "An act has been performed, and we wish to understand [consciously] how the act came about, why it came about, and what meaning we should attach to it. That is, we want to know what conclusions to draw about the future."[11] Such an assessment would be all well and good: the agent is, in his limited way, attempting a kind of science of man that we could simply term understanding or contextualizing. But such an endeavor is never exacting and the agent is often likely to be surprised at what the future holds. All the same, many things may happen that a person rightly expects to happen; it is nevertheless the case that those events are not surprising precisely because they fit into the scheme of significations by which the agent interprets his encounters. He remains attached to his own subjectivity throughout. How will we relate these thoughts on interpretation to determinism and the proposed model of the Self?

If the agent understands herself to be involved in causal connections, then the world will be interpreted in a deterministic way; i.e. certain events are interpreted as causally necessitating certain other events. At the very least, as Hume pointed out, those events are found in constant conjunction with one another.[12] Whence, then, does the idea of causation arise? Perhaps, as Locke said, it comes from the agent's own causal powers.[13] The epistemological concerns of Modern philosophy are not to be dealt with here; it is enough to elucidate the fact that an agent incorporates some notion of causation in her interpretation of events. Causality appears as a functional form of consciousness, as a way of understanding. Determinism may now look very different.

Until now the discussion has focused on the agent in a very abstract, formal sense. We have touched upon the roles of subjectivity and interpretation in the definition of agency. In order to explicate the relation of determinism and freedom to the agent we must move from the abstract to the actual. We ought now consider some individual instances of agency for this is precisely where determinism is disconcerting. When individuation is considered it becomes clear how the Self is to be made much larger than previous models have allowed and this will be the basis of its moral responsibility.

THE COMPLEX INDIVIDUATED SELF

The agent does not know nor act as an agent in general but as the specific agent that he is in himself. Here determinism can be explained in a useful manner. Return to Dennett's consideration regarding the need to interpret events. In what context does the interpretation occur? One might answer "in a subjective context," but it is not clear that such a response really says anything of use. One may go further, and be more fruitful, by saying "in a subjective context that is individuated." What would that mean?

Determinism matters to the individual subject because the interpretation of the Self requires a formulation of how the Self was determined. The question is, "What determined *me*?" It is a question of individuation. Much can be said on this point regarding personal history. Derek Parfit is famous (or infamous) for forwarding the conclusion that, "The existence of a person, during any period, just consists of the existence of his brain and body, and the thinking of his thoughts, and the doing of his deeds, and the occurrences of many other physical and mental events."[14] Parfit's view of personal identity is called reductionist. The reductionist view of personal identity will not here be endorsed. However, certain features of this view carry truth in their utility for formulating a satisfactory model of a complex, not a reduced, Self. It is a matter of convention to distinguish between physical and psychological continuity as requisites for the determination of personal identity. Parfit termed the necessary conditions of personal identity "Relation R" and defined R as "psychological connectedness and/or psychological continuity, with the right kind of cause."[15] Relation R is a useful tool in our understanding the role of determinism in the operations of agency, similar to the utility of the pragmatist's stream of consciousness account. R helps to illustrate physical and psychological continuity as a unified phenomenon, thus eliminating elements of dualism that are pervasive in philosophical debates of the twentieth century. Notice cause is not rejected as a destroyer of moral responsibility under this schemata; it is in fact necessary to individuation and, as we shall prove, to moral responsibility. The right kind of cause, for the purposes of this essay, will be those causes established in the hard sciences as necessary for the sustenance of a being displaying physical and psychological continuity; i.e. the right causes are the physiological systems that support a functional consciousness.

By positing continuity as a criterion for identity, Parfit has introduced temporality into our model. With it, unrecognized by Parfit, comes the concept of historicity.[16] The agent is entangled in the world within a certain historical context and can only interpret the world in light of that context. If consciousness is always consciousness *of* something, then it is always directed toward that of which it *is*. Intentionality comes from this directedness toward that which is perceived. The agent, aware enough of deterministic principles to question them, intuitively understands causality because it exists in a reciprocal relation with the world she perceives. Consciousness exists because this is a world that can be perceived and actions in the world produce effects that can in turn be acted on and so forth. The language of causality is explicitly temporal because it is a series—implying that behind the causal description lies a temporality over the duration of which the causal chain unfolds. Thus, we derive continuity. For the agent, identity becomes the Relation R and R's unique history—the historicity of R. A historical narrative could be built around the agent on many levels, that of the nation, the species, the family, the public, the private. At the nexus of all of these narratives, that, if she were to speak, would deliver a first person account of said narratives, is an individuated self, an "I" subject. If Relation R constitutes the subject then it is only Relation R *as interpreted by the subject that experiences the relationships*. That the interpretation is the subject's own is not relevant for reasons of such an interpretation's accuracy or truth-value. The subject's own interpretation is essential because consciousness, when conscious of herself as consciousness, appears as other to herself. The mistaken assumption of an identical self-presence results when we wrongly assign ontological significances equivalent to extension or object-like existence to the intentionality we direct toward ourselves as entities in the world. Thus, the agent is a being 1) in a reciprocal causal relationship with herself as with the world, and 2) as such, causally responsible for herself as an entity in the world. What makes the agent unique is her awareness of her constitutive historicity as that historicity is given to her.[17]

The Self is becoming sufficiently complex. Everything within the agent's field of consciousness is a potential causal force, including all of those things regarding himself that he perceives. Reason, emotion, desires, intentions, are modes of the agent's interaction with and interpretation of his experiences in the world. These factors act functionally for Relation R to obtain between the subjective and the objective. The question remains, "how is the agent free?" In this model of the Self, causal relations are important; they cannot be negated, reduced, or ignored. There is room also for the agent to do some work and possibly to be morally responsible for the work that he does. It will be shown how complexity will aid in this work without stranding the agent in an indeterministic trap.[18]

FREE ACTS WITHIN THE MODEL

A commonly argued refutation of indeterminist principles states that indeterminism amounts to something that is random and therefore no better than mere luck or chance.[19] Parallels have been drawn between indeterministic decision-making and random number generation.[20] Such parallels are intended to the detriment of an indeterminist position as espoused by Robert Kane.

Comparisons between the agent and a random number generator are actually quite apt, not because the agent is random, but because the agent is *unpredictable*. Computer science has come a long way in the development of random and quasi-random number generators whose explicit purpose is unpredictability, or indeterminate results. From this it follows that the functions of a random number generator, how it works to produce a random number, are not at all mysterious, nor unfathomable. Still, the output of the random number generator cannot be predicted due to the very nature of these functions. The same could be said of the agent.

Historicity can only account for a part of the agent's identity, the part that is in the past with experiences and encounters that have already occurred and been interpreted. Thus, this past, which has become an object of the understanding, obtains a determined significance. The future remains open and *yet to be determined*. The agent does this determinative work, and both determinist and indeterminist views gloss over this important work. Determinism insists that such work is done, but that the work is entirely external to the agent. Indeterminism wants the agent to do work, but deprives the agent of her ability to do work by removing her from the causal chain, placing her within the same dilemma as the determinists—causality becomes pure exteriority. Both views fall prey to the same error in reasoning. A correction of that error shows freedom's place in the model of the Self forwarded here.

The error lies in how these views explain the relationship between the act and the subject. The error implies dualism that separates the agent from his actions. The separation permits the agent no claim on his actions. On both accounts, there exists a real and meaningful distinction between "merely immanent" or "intentional" objects and the "transcendent," "actual" objects that correspond to those intentions, which appear as signs to the conscious subject. Take a simple case, one of little controversy. A person wishes to cross the street. They are going somewhere, perhaps to the post office in order to ship a package. On his way, the agent needs to cross a busy intersection. The agent stops at the corner to wait for the proper signal that it is safe to cross. He is aware of cars passing by, of other pedestrians, of the traffic light across the street that indicates an appropriate time for him to cross, and of many things inconsequential to his intentions such as the fact that the sun is shining or that a bird is pecking the ground nearby. The philosopher's error occurs when an account of this agent and his intention to ship a package gets broken down into a dualism of physical immanence and immaterial transcendence. There then exists a real and meaningful difference between the traffic light that is the object of the agent's intentions and the traffic light that transcends those intentions in the objective sense that it exists "out there," in the world. There are two ways of phrasing the error, one in which the distinction is made between a sign or image present in consciousness and the thing for which that sign or image stands, and the other in which sense data of the content of consciousness is substituted for the object of intention.[21] Deterministic views tend to err in the first way, while indeterminist views err more commonly in the latter. Determinism holds that external causal forces determine the action of the agent while the agent's experience of those factors is a mere chimera upon which the agent cannot act on his own, or, if the agent does act, his actions are nothing more than the unfolding of effects of external causal forces. Indeterminism holds that the agent receives data regarding his encounters in the world and forms intentions as a result of this sense data but that the agent is not of the same nature as the objects about which it receives sense data, and so the agent is not encountering the object itself but, once again, a chimera that is representing a real object to his consciousness.

The dualism is a false one. The agent is encountering objects that exist alongside her in the objective world. Husserl stated the resolution this way: "*that the intentional object of a presentation is the same as the actual object, and on occasion its external object, and that it is absurd to distinguish between them.*"[22] The objective entity in the world, the one encountered by the agent and that consciousness presents as affectation, would not be the object of the agent's intention if it were not simultaneously the entity that the agent encountered in the world. Intention means and refers to that real entity which is presented by consciousness. If we say that an intentional object exists, that object does not exist by itself; the entity that is referred to by intentionality must exist also, in some form, or intentionality would be devoid of that toward which it intends. Returning to the proposed model of the Self it is clear why the dissolution of dualism is both effective and logical.

The resulting agent turns intentionality on himself, as he does he recognizes his own consciousness, thus the intentional object becomes the Self—the Self that is an actual entity in the world alongside other objects that he encounters. How is this entity presented? Relation R is one possibility for this presentation. But it can only be this Relation in terms of the agent's singular historicity. Any so-called "Cartesian Theatre," that locus of selfhood "where it all comes together,"[23] appears empty not only because there is no imaginary homunculus that is distributed in time and space within the brain, the Theatre is empty because the Self is not a static, objective locality within the body—the Self is, in part, selfsame as the body. The Self is the unfolding of the subjective experience of that embodied entity as he comes to interpret himself as an entity in the world. It is becoming and as such is only partially disclosed as determined by historicity.

The example of a person attempting to cross the street utilizes a real entity in the world. The person is there, on the street corner experiencing a traffic signal (and all manner of other phenomena) that is also there and is the object of said person's intentions. Determinists maintain that the person waits on the corner because the "Do not cross" sign causally determines that the person wait until the perception of the "Cross" signal initiates a series of events in the brain that causally determine the person to cross the street. The determinist explanation fails to account for the functions of a person and her conscious agency. The view is far too simplistic having totally lost sight of the historicity that individuates each person. The leading up to the crossing of the street could be narrated by an internalized monologue of thought processes unfolding in a person's mind as they decide on crossing the street: *I have to deliver this package and so I'm going to go to the post office today around one, after I've had lunch. I'll eat at the deli on __ Street, it's right by the post office and that will be easier than walking across town during lunch traffic. The intersection at __ Street is always busy, I'll probably have to wait there a while. I better not dilly-dally so I can make it back to work on time*—and so forth. Notice first the variety of considerations that might go into making any given decision, even, or especially, very simple ones such as crossing the street.

Then consider: the agent for whom it is possible to wait on the corner for a light to change must have already incorporated the meaning of the light into her decision-making process *before* she actually encountered the light at the corner. So, when the traffic light is in fact encountered, her understanding of traffic law and the direction of her movement prior to her encountering the traffic signal allow her to make certain decisions regarding how she will interpret the signal. When the light is encountered it is determined a priori by the agent's cognitive understanding of "red light" and that this means to stop, just as a green light means "go." She intuitively navigates pedestrian and vehicular traffic and comprehends the difference between the two, and also what a post office is, what the function of money is, that crossing the street is potentially dangerous, that one ought take care when traveling from place to place, and so on until the totality of consciousness be fleshed out according, maybe, to Relation R, or some other mode of discussing the singularity of historicity. It is the agent that determines the traffic signal upon encountering it, not the other way around, as the determinists would have us suppose. The agent determined "if the signal is red, then I shall stop and wait" before she ever arrived at the signal so that when she eventually did encounter the light the agent freely waited by her own determination. The agent may just have well decided "I'm in a hurry, so green signal or not, I'm crossing the street." In this case, the signal would have been disregarded as a causal factor. Perhaps in reality the vehicular traffic at the intersection was so busy that the person was in fact unable to cross the street with disregard for the signal. In a case such as this, with busy traffic, it would be the severity of the traffic itself, in conjunction with the strength of the agent's will to live that determined she would not cross the street, not the indications of the signal itself.

How exactly can these kinds of actions be free? Some philosopher's will likely not be satisfied with the account I offer thus far. Complete philosophical satisfaction is nigh impossible to come by. Despite that, further elucidation on how freedom functions in the proposed model will here be attempted. In summary of the previous arguments, it must be said that freedom, as it is understood so far, occurs because the agent is himself doing some causal work. He is not separate from the causal chain and is, at times, certainly a "victim" of causal factors that are beyond his control. However, the agent is aware of causal factors and of his place among them and even understands causality itself due, in part, to his own causal powers. It was shown how an agent could determine the significance of an object such as a traffic signal by his cognition of the world in advance of his encounter with a particular object—in our example, the traffic signal. These preceding considerations are to be applied to a theory of freedom and responsibility.

HOW COMPLEXITY SETS THE AGENT FREE

A great deal has been made of the agent's complexity. The bulk of this essay has concerned itself with explaining the insufficiency of a simple model of the Self. A simple model is insufficient not only in explaining agency itself, but in understanding the relations involved in causal connections, especially when some of these connections are known to the agent. This is not to say that the agent knows *all* causal factors, only that she knows *some*, even a small fraction of them. In fact, it is entirely possible that the agent be mistaken about some of the causal connections she recognizes. The agent could not possibly be expected to account for all causal factors that come to bear on a particular decision. The number would be so vast as to be an astronomical sum. So the question becomes, "Which causal connections are important?" Even better, "Are any of these causal connections important?" The answers to these questions are "it depends" and "it depends," respectively. On what does such a thing depend? Very naturally, it depends on the agent.

Complexity supports the arguments in favor of freedom in a few ways. For one, there are such a huge number of causal connections involved that what it is that exactly necessitates a given action is not a problem for the agent's freedom. The answer is arbitrary. What would determine any one connection or set of connections to be favored as causally necessitating a particular action? Are all connections necessitating? That does not seem to make intuitive sense. Many of the causal connections the agent is aware of have no real bearing on the situation in which she must decide. If the focus is shifted to those that do in fact bear on the situation the number is still vast. The number remains vast, not because of all the causal connections converging in the moment, but because, since the agent is involved, all of the causal connections converging in the moment are brought into conjunction with all of those connections which make up the singular historicity of the individuated agent. Again, which causes are necessitating? Not all of them. Not all of them are even relevant. It is true that there may be some relevant connections that are surprising, and some that may be unknown, but that does not imply that all relations bear on all decisions at every moment. The Kantian approach serves us well here, because determinism attempts to make all causal connections necessary events and thereby formulate predictions regarding the agent's decisions. Under the Kantian approach the so-called science of man is denied. Given the model of the Self that has been explored in this essay the reasons why there is no science of man should be clear. Under the proposed conception the causally necessitating factors cannot be isolated from Relation R's supposed totality, and thus is inevitably a false objectification.

There are external causal factors and internal causal factors. The terminology is a mixed blessing. It will be shown how "internal" and "external" are not to be taken in a literal, i.e. spatial, sense. In this instance, "external" factors are all those factors that are not involved with the agent until the time of her decision-making. Internal factors, then, are those composing the constitution of the agent at the time of her decision-making. Recall the previous comparisons to random number generators. The decision of the agent is not random; it is unpredictable. It is unpredictable because all those causal factors that go into the make-up of a person cannot be isolated by any objective observer and laid out for analysis. Some factors may be very well known, but they may not be the relevant ones, or they may not be the totality of relevant ones, or some other possible epistemic configuration.[24] Thus, the crucial moment of the agent's enacted freedom.

The relevance of causal connection is dependent on the agent, because it is the agent's own interpretation of his historicity that is utilized in the formation of conscious decisions. When the agent engages in a conscious, deliberative process it is determining the significance of the factors being taken into consideration This is, in part, the causal work the agent does; it determines which strains of causal connections are going to be the basis of her decisions. These become the agent's reasons for acting when her actions are conscious. Part of the agent's unpredictability stems from her individuation. Her interpretation is her own and her significations are formed according to a historicity that is her own and to which she has privileged access. Other people can know *about* that unique historicity, but no other person has experience of it and cannot, therefore, determine which causal factors are necessitating. The agent necessitates by choosing those causal connections on which to act. If the Self was a simple self, it could not be able to do this because large parts of what constitutes a criterion like Relation R (beliefs, desires, reasons, wants, etc.) do not belong to the agent.

Under the complex view, those things do belong to the agent, but moreover, the agent does causal work with them. Remember, the agent is posited here as existing in a reciprocal causal relationship with the world she encounters.

OWNERSHIP AND RESPONSIBILITY

The agent understands his relationship with the world by labeling his experiences as "mine." An "I" subject understands criteria like Relation R as being his own, as "my Relation R; my life, my history." He claims ownership of those things in his understanding of himself and in the way he presents himself in the world. The agent understands himself to have made a decision, "It was *my* decision." No amount of philosophical argumentation can strip this fact from the world. It could be articulated in a logical form, but such articulations would amount to mere sophistry. Subjectivity claims ownership of himself through his interpretation of his encounters in the world. The subject can understand his experiences in no other terms than those that imply ownership of the experiences by the subject.

It could be argued that the agent does not really "own" her experiences so to speak; she only appears to in formal articulations of herself. If this is the case, then there is no agent. The whole free will debate is a practice in deterministic futility. There is no agent, no freedom, and no responsibility. If such is that case, who is carrying on this debate? How is it even possible to debate, to speak, to listen, or to react? Who is this speaker that speaks and listens without action, without responding, without the possibility of responsibility and thus without the ability to respond? Earlier there had been discussion regarding the object of intentionality being identical with objects in the world. If there is no agent, of what then is self-consciousness conscious of? Of what is she aware when she considers freedom, or responsibility in turn? Critics could say she is actually aware of nothing and reinforce the immanence/transcendence dichotomy. But it could then be shown how nothing is really something.

According to Sartre, for instance, being aware of one's own nothingness would mean to be aware of one's own-most potentiality for being.[25] The potential for a continuation of Relation R in the future, the Self as projected into a future that is, to the Self, unknown until it is encountered, until the experience of it. But the agent has intentions toward a goal set in that unknown future. Such goals can only be determined by the Self because the future is undisclosed to the agent as it will be determined. As it is, the future is not yet determined and only takes on a predetermined significance once the agent has encountered and determined it within her singular historicity. Hence, even the undisclosed future is a future that could be one's own; it is sensible to talk about "my future." This talk of nothingness is treading too close to the radical, irresponsible freedom espoused by Sartre. The crucial parallel is this: the agent is not an object in the sense that a chair, book, or rock is an object. The agent has a body, and perhaps that body can be objectified in a sense, but that body is only an aspect of continuity. The body is changing, mobile, self-exploratory, and given her consciousness, axiomatic in a way that rocks are not.

A person is not radically free in Sartre's sense precisely because of his historicity. He did not choose where and when to be born. But this entity that he enters the world without choice is born into a world in which he must eventually choose. He develops a robust awareness of himself that opens him to possibility. There comes to be a horizon of choice available to the agent as he develops self-consciousness. Awareness of one's own historicity presents a distance from that historicity and brings causality under the intentional direction of consciousness. He does not become responsible for himself and for his actions merely by understanding his own role in the connections formed by causality. Rather, he becomes aware that he is always already responsible whether he knows it or not, for responsibility cannot be taken away from the agent; it is one of his modes of being in the world. His responsibility can only be overshadowed by factors that the agent is unable to distance himself from and interprets as necessitating one particular action over others within his horizon of choice. Moral culpability might be excused in such instances, but the agent may still incur shame upon himself. He will still claim ownership of his actions, even of those actions that he perceives as being necessitated by forces exterior to himself. He understands his own responsibility in terms of determinism and causality. Specifically, in terms of causation, which he interprets as his own, and that result in determined events beyond the agent's immediate actions in the world. Determinism, then, is essential to moral responsibility.

DETERMINED RESPONSIBILITY AND MORAL CULPABILITY

The agent interprets past events under a scheme of determinism and causality. In projecting herself into the future she carries this understanding with her in order to execute her plans. Accomplishing a goal depends on a certain level of predictability regarding one's own actions. This is not equivalent to a science of man. Anyone who has formulated a plan and executed it knows fully well how things can go wrong, or not quite as expected. Sometimes, events do go according to plan and a deep feeling of satisfaction wells up within the agent. But it must be stressed that, even in instances where a plan unfolds "without a hitch" the unfolding of that event in the world does not correspond exactly to the imagined vision of that event as projected by the individual. There exist inconsequential discrepancies between the person's imagining of a future event and the event as it unfolds as a result of her conscious efforts. This is no cause for alarm and often is expected by an agent who knows that complete predictability is an epistemological impossibility. If events were indeterminate, there would be no reason for praise or blame, no room for moral judgments or responsibility.

Agents involved in interpersonal relations must have an intuitive understanding of causality that extends from his actions into the unknown future. If the agent did not expect determinism to obtain as a result of his actions there would be no ground on which to hold one another morally culpable. There would be no causal link between a person's actions and the consequences for which society holds them accountable. Determinism must hold in some sense or moral responsibility is unintelligible. The determinism that holds is determinism in the sense discussed in the foregoing sections on agency. There is one more issue at hand that leads us finally to the conclusion of our work on moral responsibility and determinism. Again, the issue arises from the complexity of the Self, out of the fact that the Self is no longer so small.

If the Self is expanded to fill a criterion such as Relation R, she must take account of others. Agency exists alongside other agents and is conscious of the existence of these agents as an agent herself. As such, others constitute part of what the agent is in herself, even beyond her mere external relations to them; for we all share experiences that are mutually formative of our physical and psychological continuities and aid in the reciprocating individuation of one another. As an agent is morally responsible for herself, she is also, though perhaps to a lesser degree, morally responsible for the others as well. Proximity to others increases mutual responsibility as the agents become more and more identified with one another. Though no two agents can ever be identical with one another, nevertheless, they may share in a relation to such an extent that they are able to interpret and predict one another's actions much better than is generally possible. The interrelationship amounts to a capability of giving an account of a person's actions that is as close to that person's own first-hand account as is possible. Such interrelationship would hold in the face of even the most annihilating interpretations of determinism. Though such interpretations of determinism are wildly inaccurate, they are utilized by many schools of thought as excuses for behavior that is otherwise seen as morally apprehensible. Under the conception put forth in this essay, though actions may be excused or acquitted, there remains responsibility, thus moral culpability. The relations under which this culpability holds was expressed succinctly by Camus when he writes,

> At this limit "we are" paradoxically defines a new form of individualism. "We are" in terms of history, and history must reckon with "We are," which must in turn keep its place in history…Every collective action, every form of society, supposes a discipline, and the individual, without this discipline, is a stranger, bowed down under the weight of an inimical collectivity.[26]

In the proposed view, historicity is reconciled with the agent, individuating him while at once freeing him in the world to act from his own subjectivity. Consciousness of freedom, and of moral responsibility, is a recognition of the agent's own actions in the world and a claim of ownership on those actions that hold each individual agent to those others alongside which he exists as an entity in the world. His modalities of being are concrete, not as objects, but as relations that obtain between objective and subjective and are dispersed throughout time.

TWO BRIEF APOLOGIES

Before any concluding remarks can be made, there must be forwarded an explanation regarding certain assumptions held by the arguments in this paper.

The first is simply that determinism is not God-like. Problems arising for freedom from the theistic view occur because of God's foreknowledge. God knew what would happen before it happened because he was the prime cause of all things that happened. There was no causality outside of God.

Determinism, on the other hand, is not a conscious force, as is the popular conception of God. Deterministic principles do not know the consequences to which they will lead. Principles of determinism are not "responsible" for events in this way. They are blind to any plan that may be projected into the future. In this sense, determined events just happen. This is not to say that they have no causes, only that they have no reasons, as agents do.

That said, it is also the case that the model of the Self recommended in this paper is working under atheistic assumptions. The model may be compatible with theistic views in some way, but it is the author's view that the existence of a personal God (as proposed by traditional Judeo-Christian theology) poses very serious problems for an agent's freedom. There is no successful argument, again, in the author's reasoned view, which has yet proven how a person can be free under the dominion of an almighty personal God. Although the Sartrean radical freedom is rejected, Sartre's atheistic conclusions are accepted; if God exists man is not free.

An argument for or against the existence of a personal God was not the project of this paper although there are some very good reasons to hold the opinion that God does not exist in the form conceived by traditional Judeo-Christian theology. Admittedly, there are good reasons to maintain that there is a personal God; the author simply reasons that these arguments fail in light of his own experiences in the world and given the logical inconsistencies inherent in any ontology composed of fundamentally exclusive dualities or other divisive dichotomies.

Given the restraints of time and length provided for in this essay and the already formidable task set out in its thesis, the issue of theism as it relates to the theories entailed therein could not be adequately addressed. In an effort not to ignore them, those issues are acknowledge here though they cannot be handled with the detail they rightfully deserve.

These apologies made, the time is right for some concluding remarks.

CONCLUSION

Determinism, freedom, and moral responsibility are all concepts that are essential to a person's understanding of the world. The concepts constitute certain significances without which the agent would fail to render any sensible interpretation of the world. All of them seem tied irrevocably to the very being of the agent herself, and result from the functions of consciousness and its relation to the world. There may be a theoretical denial of the existence of the proposed conceptualization, but the direct experience of these relations in the world reveal such denials in their sophistry. The question for analytics comes down to what these concepts mean and it is only the shifting definitions of those concepts that has lead to their mutual exclusivity. Once the blinders of mere systemization are shed and the phenomenological motto of "to the things themselves" is adopted it becomes clear that the questions of the metaphysics of freedom are not at all metaphysical. The questions regard personhood, what a person is, and how she acts in the world. It could be seen as ontological. Perhaps the ontology of freedom is a more apt pursuit than is the metaphysics of freedom. In the end, it depends, as has been shown, on the inquirer. So, the beginning is found again here, in the end, and the hermeneutics of the issue is again reinforced. What is sought guides the seeking and the Self is revealed in its axiomatic subjectivity.

Notes to The Possibility of Responsible Freedom

[1] Leo Tolstoy, *War and Peace*, trans. Richard Pevear & Larissa Volokhonsky, (New York: Random House, 2007), 506.

[2] Chisholm, "Human Freedom…" 134.

[3] Ibid. 133.

[4] Ibid. 126.

[5] My essay "The Ontological I," presented in the current volume, argues a more complete theory of personal identity.

[6] Note my particular use of the term "metaphysics," outlined on pages 15, and 54—56 of the current volume.

[7] See for example, Jean-Paul Sartre, *Being and Nothingness*, trans. Hazel Barnes, (New York: Washington Square Press, 1992), 11.

[8] Husserl, *Logical Investigations vol. 1*, trans. (New York: Routledge, 2001), 77.

[9] See the prolegomena to the current work. To be clear, that argument stated that Chisholm had inadvertently made all things external to the agent, thus the entire causal chain became pure exteriority. Being indeterminate, this model of the self has no way to act and is rendered powerless by its own disconnection from causality. Chisholm, by making the agent a prime mover unmoved, neglected the possibility that a part of the causality constituting the agent is a part of the agent itself. The implications of this argument will be fleshed out in the present argument.

[10] Dennett, *Elbow Room: Varieties of Free Will Worth Having*, (Cambridge. MA: The MIT Press, 1984), 143.

[11] Ibid. 142.

[12] Hume, "An Inquiry Concerning Human Understanding." *The Empiricists*, (New York: Random House, 1990), 351.

[13] Locke, "An Essay Concerning Human Understanding: abridged." *The Empiricists*, (New York: Random House, 1990), 42.

[14] Parfit, *Reasons and Persons*, (New York: Oxford University Press, 1987), 275.

[15] Ibid. 262.

[16] This term has been in currency for some time, notable for our purposes in Hegel, Schopenhauer, and Heidegger, but it is not the author's intention to invoke any one of their specific definitions for the term. Appropriately, it is the 'spirit' of the term, so to speak, that is invoked here. Discussion regarding the effects of social conditioning, education, social class, and heredity on the development of a human being has been cast in a certain language favorable to the assumptions of hard determinism. Historicity will serve to better express the authors meaning.

[17] See, for instance, Heidegger, *Being and Time*, trans. (San Francisco, CA: Harper Collins, 1962), 32.

[18] It is common for Indeterminism to be reducible to some theory that "the act, or some event essential to the act, is not caused at all" [Chisholm, "Human Freedom and the Self." 126]. Other common formulations explain, "'indeterminism' is a technical term that merely precludes *deterministic* causation (though not causation altogether," [Robert Kane, "Responsibility, Luck and Chance: Reflections on Free Will and Indeterminism." *Agency and Responsibility*, ed. Laura Waddell Ekstrom, (Boulder, CO: Westview Press, 2001), 163]. The trap is that these accounts of indeterminism tend to weaken the work done by the agent enough to undermine the arguments for that agent's freedom and responsibility.

[19] Such is the argument found in: Kane, "Responsibility, Luck and Chance." 158—80. Kane is himself an indeterminist and is explaining here the most common objection to his views.

[20] Notably at: Daniel Dennett, *Freedom Evolves*, (New York: Penguin Putnam, 2003), 112.

[21] In general, this represents a refutation of a *representational* model of perception. A similar one is forwarded by Husserl, *Logical Investigations, vol. 2*, trans. (New York: Routledge, 2001), 126.

[22] Ibid. 126. The italics are Husserl's own; this was a solution he was quite impressed with.
[23] Dennet, *Freedom Evolves*, 123.
[24] This is not an argument against determinism on the grounds of epistemological uncertainty. If hard determinism holds to the extent that an agent is not morally responsible, then that determinism will obtain regardless of humanity's epistemological prowess. In fact, this is not really an argument against determinism at all. It is an argument against determinism causally necessitating the decisions of an agent. The decisions are caused, but they are not necessitated before they occur. The future is open. Complexity provides for that.
[25] Sartre, *Being and Nothingness*, 126.
[26] Camus, *The Rebel*, 297.

ETHICS IN REBELLION

The question of ethics is often a question of right, both political and personal. The question of right forces us to consider the possibility of an objectively true value system by which we could discerned a criteria for absolute rights. Ethics thus implies an epistemological dimension. The epistemological questions appear, phenomenologically, as uncertainty or doubt concerning ethics when we are called upon to validate an ethical claim. Therefore, it would be prudent to analyze a possible source of ethical values to determine what the nature of the values produced by this source might be and whether or not we might reasonably argue for the acceptance of these supposed values. One possible source of ethical values is the human condition, and it is this source that we concern ourselves with in this essay. Within the human condition, a being, the human being, through his or her actions, formulates and validates their own ethical claims. The anthropogenic enquiry is necessary because the inquiry into the question of what one ought to do answers the question of what one ought to do by the very inquiry. What one ought to do is inquire; and this is to inquire of the inquirer what her own limitations are. What better way to discern what one ought to do than by the way that leads to the discovery of what one is in oneself, thereby discovering the limits of one's own being?

Consider the human being that "objects to" some condition of his existence. The objection to one's condition is ethical because it asserts that what ought to be the case is not, in fact, the case. It appeals to a moral order; that an injustice is being incurred by the very conditionality of my own-most being. To wage a rebellion against these very conditions of our reality is to wage a war against a moral invasion that is deemed to be intolerable and due the violence of resistance against this intrusion. The rejection of the world is founded upon the ideal of rights, a confusion regarding the nature of right, and what is, in the mind of the rebellious, the notion that he has any "right to" the freedom to act in accordance with his own will. Thus, in affirmation of the absolute personal right, the rebel categorically rejects the intrusion of the conditions of his existence on his personal freedom.

How is it that an individual discerns her values? Is it possible for an individual to appeal to absolute right if it is not clear that such a thing as absolute right exists in the first place? The epistemic question asks for an examination of what is known about the self and the conditions in which selves are found.

Specifically, what is it about an individual's condition that inspires the negation of one value system in favor of another. After all, if a value system is one thing, then there are necessarily value systems that the chosen one is not, and thus other possible value systems that are not, in fact, in operation by the individual. Camus would respond that "He [the rebel] opposes the principle of justice which he finds in himself to the principle of injustice which he sees being applied in the world."[1] However, in Camus' analysis, there is a relationship between the rebel and his rejection of values that is polarizing. The individual and the universe are polarized so that the individual's perception of their self is one of total isolation. When we try to analyze the truth or the falsehood of moral values, we are looking into the consequences of the relationships of a plurality of individuals living in a mutually perceived world; we are looking at a world that is shared.

Once the inter-relational aspect of the inquiry becomes obvious, subjective perceptions become emphasized. It is the experiences perceived within the mutual world, which caused discrepancies between the individual and the universe. Between, again, the principle of justice which one finds in oneself and the principle of injustice which one sees enacted in the world. Once formulated in this way, the ethics appears to have strongly empirical elements. There is thus a method by which individuals utilize their empirical knowledge to make value judgments, particularly, for the purposes of the current inquiry, judgments concerning the nature of the self.

David Hume's thesis that there is no persistent, objective self that is the subject of experience—though there must be a formal or logical requirement that such a self is postulated as something in addition to the experiences themselves—has been greatly expanded upon by thinker's throughout the twentieth century. It is common to refer to theorists following the logic of Hume to an extreme as "reductionist" because of their tendency to reduce the self to brain states, mental or physical continuity with the right kind of cause, or some other function of biology, physiology, et cetera. The specific problem with following Hume's theory too dogmatically lies in Hume's theory of perception, which was greatly improved by Kant. Hume claimed that experiences came to the individual in discrete units he called "impressions" or "ideas" although actual lived experience presents as a more or less continuous and unified field of perceptions—the so-called manifold. A further problem appears when we consider the logical necessity of postulating a subject, in requiring the concept of self, any time we wish to deal with experience, perception, or other such philosophical topics.

If it is *necessary* to postulate a self, some identity, then that identity that is called the self must carry out a systematic function that is not reducible to brain states or other such biological or physiological phenomenon. Rather, the resort to brain states and other such explanations further strengthens this necessity. It is precisely by brain states and the like that the self is explained and supported, but these reductions do not point to that which the self *is*. Correlation is not identification. Because brain state A coincides with mental state A the two are not necessarily one and the same. The correlation may give rise to explanation regarding causation or interrelation, but it does not reinforce the notion of identity. In fact, by the very possibility of correlation, it is shown that there are two separate things in play, brain states *and* mental states—which happen to be correlated.

Attempts have been made to account for the appearance of a subjective reference. For instance, Michel Foucault explored "three modes of objectification that transform human beings into subjects."[2] This transformation into a subject carries two meanings: the first, in which one becomes subject to someone else qua control and dependence, and a second, whereby one becomes bound to a static identity through self-knowledge and conscience—and these two meanings are, for Foucault, indicative of powers that would "subjecgate," or "make subject to." Objectified people are placed within complex social relationships that are based on an imbalance of power between individuals. From such a perspective we can hypothesize that it is precisely these power relations against which the individual rebels. The individual's renunciation of the role assigned to them within the social power structure implies the affirmation of their absolute right against the violation of that right by the limitation power places on their autonomy. It is the context in which the individual is defined that inspires the negation.

Rebellion against modes of objectification calls into question the validity of the "individual-as-object" formulation of selfhood. A reexamination of the definition of the individual as an object within a set of power relations is in order. All power struggles here originate with the question, "who am I?" while simultaneously refusing those abstractions that ignore the personal, subjective nature of selfhood.[3] Dissent thus attempts to affirm existence and empower it.

Nietzsche might have called this the Will to Power—when the individual struggles to redefine their relation to the objective world as a subject. The aim would be to, as Foucault put it, "promote new forms of subjectivity through the refusal of this kind of individuality that has been imposed...for several centuries."[4] That is, the refusal of the subject-as-object scheme. Indeed, it is the conception of the self as "bad" or of lesser moral value that is so offensive to the person in rebellion. The examples given by Camus all seek elevation to a higher level of moral worth. The slave wishes to equal the master, the metaphysical rebel to equal God, the historical rebel to equal the king, and the artist rebel deigns to create her own reality.[5] It was Nietzsche who pointed out this fundamental problem with the popular conception of good and evil when he analyzed the etymological significance of the words used to mean "good." He writes:

> ...*the same evolution of the same idea*—that everywhere "aristocrat," "noble" (in the social sense), is the root idea, out of which have necessarily developed "good" in the sense of "with aristocratic soul," "noble," in the sense of "with a soul of higher caliber," "with a privileged soul"—a development which invariable runs parallel with that other evolution by which "vulgar," "plebian," "low" are made to change finally into "bad."[6]

Nietzsche is describing the moral imposition of value onto a social relation of power that effectively ignores the individuality of the individual in favor of canvassing hierarchies of moral worth on the social order. Against objectification is the anarchic reaction that questions the status of the individual within the social order. The

Will to Power becomes the struggle to define one's own status in the world. A step toward enabling this re-assignment of status is a redefinition of the subject as non-object. Thus, any so-called objective definition of the subject must account for its subjectivity, instead of imposing object-like definitions on the subject-like reality of the self.

The conflict occurs between the subjectivity that the person is in and of herself and the consequences of being identified as an object in a process of objectification. One possibility is that any given person cannot be separated from the context in which their experiences are perceived because of the affect these experiences produce on the determination of the individual's identity. If such were the case, rebellion amounts to the rejection of values imposed over the freedom of an individual to act autonomously; thus, *to be defined by experiences brought about by their own will.* What is required is a revision of the basic concept of personhood as postulated by Hume that permits the subject to be self-determined instead of being valuated from an exteriority. The solution to this need of revision lies in a critique of the philosophy of Kant.

One reductionistic philosopher that always comes to the fore of my mind is Derek Parfit. He claims that a person is the psychological continuity of a subject of perception with the right kind of cause.[7] His argument concludes that, "The existence of a person, during any period, just consists in the existence of his brain and body, and the thinking of his thoughts, and the doing of his deeds, and the occurrence of many other physical and mental events."[8] To posit *continuity* as a criterion for identity better fulfills the conditions of actual experience as a manifold than did Hume's confused notions regarding impressions. Further, Parfit is attempting to account for the turn of perception toward that which perceives. This resonates with a philosopher such as John Searle, who wants to argue that when a consciousness turns perception in on itself, it perceives nothing but a sequence of experiences which it has stored by way of memory and which it can relate to the general timeline of the consciousness' experience.[9] Although it is tempting to objectify the individual as some sort of point of perception, or as an object passing through a stream of time, this would be an abuse of language. There is basis for a systematic de-objectification. First, by removing the mysterious "further fact" from the equation of identity, at which most reductionists make a bold attempt. Secondly, we allow the person to be a dynamic system, that is, a process of becoming—an aggregate of continuous experience. The intrusion of external values could be eliminated, permitting a healthy, functioning individual to be the constant redefinition of himself, sometimes in spite of his condition. But such liberation would not be possible while the fetters of the power relation blind to the subjective self remain intact.

Consider relationships wherein an individual is subjugated by another individual or by a collective. The subjugated individual comes to recognize the discrepancies between its own belief in personal justice and the injustice it perceives in the world and thus formulates value judgments in opposition to the world. But the negative values system has arisen from a perceived injustice and so must carry injustice with it until the rebellious soul embraces injustice as the instrument of her liberation. Thus the rebel who continues to objectify herself even as they negate the exterior objectification can only perpetuate that selfsame objectification. If it is assumed then, that others share their mode of being, the rebel will inevitably come to objectify the other by epistemic extension.

A problem crystallizes: that the individual has been defined as having access to *a priori* knowledge of justice that is not empirical knowledge. Classical ontology postulates *a priori* knowledge as part and parcel of individuality; *a priori* knowledge is part of the individual's being as an object. It is precisely this *a priori* conception of justice that the empirical world of experience fails to match. In the Platonic dialogues, Socrates forces the interlocutors beyond what they had held to be self-evident in order to discover an objective truth inherent in the universe that would illuminate their perceptions from within. Socrates is presented as being concerned with what *is* in the same way that Camus' rebel concerns herself with what *is*; both perceive the world of being incapable of meeting the ideal of justice that they find within themselves.

But neither Plato nor Socrates are quite rebels in Camus' sense of the term. Plato is perhaps best described as a revolutionary. He is the rebel who carries on the scheme of objectification. Camus adheres to the astronomical concept of revolution as a full cycle. Revolution revolves in a complete rotation back to the origin.[10] Socrates would not dream of overthrowing the ideal of justice. He is trying to replace the existing notions held by the interlocutors with a different conception of the same categorical object. He wants to bring them around to a re-conceptualization of the justice in the

Good. The rebel in Camus' sense wants a new ontology of justice. In Plato, there is no reconciliation of the power relationships that give Camus' rebel his sense of violation. In fact, Plato seems to uphold those despotic power relations in Book VII of the *Republic* when he writes, "that it's not the concern of law that any one class in the city fare exceptionally well, but it contrives to bring this about in the city as a whole, harmonizing the citizens by persuasion and compulsion, making them share with one another the benefit that each is able to bring to the commonwealth."[11] This amounts to an endorsement of the intrusion on absolute right that serves as the very impetus to the rebel's revolt. The contradiction is reinforced. On the one hand, Plato is arguing for a kind of harmony, which the rebel may find to be desirable, seeking as he does a reconciliation of his own sense of justice and that justice which he wishes to manifest in the world. However, this harmony is a harmony of coercion, which is the intrusion that the rebel has rejected. The citizens are made to share; that is, they are not really sharing, they are the victims of systematic appropriation and subjugation to the "citizen-subject" which is forced into the hierarchy by persuasion and compulsion.

It is Plato's view, however, that if those in the position to intrude upon individual rights are philosophers, then they will be in a position to know the Good and thus ensure that their intrusions are truly just, avoiding the discrepancies in power which would drive an individual into a state of rebellion.[12] Socrates harbors no skepticism regarding the epistemological possibility of good and evil. Plato's dialogues are an endless sacrifice of Sophist values to the idol of Truth. The egoism of the Socratic character in Platonic dialogues will not admit a fundamental discrepancy in the human condition, only discreet discrepancies between individual perceptions and the actuality of the ground of the Forms. By focusing on what does not change, "on that which is illuminated by truth and that which *is*, it intellects, it knows, and appears to possess intelligence."[13]

A Platonist trusts that the perception can be focused on a constant Form that will bring objective illumination to their subjective perceptions. But Camus had pointed out that the rebel had a "confused conviction" concerning absolute right.[14] It is possible that justice is not admissible as an *a priori* concept of the mind. The concept of justice is formed over time as a consequence of an individual's experience of practical justice in the world. It is the attempt by the individual to enter into a dialectical assessment of the just by comparing their own developmental ideas with the concept appearing in exteriority. This dialectical movement between ideality and actuality generates the conflict between the personal conception of justice and the injustice apparent in the world. Kant, whose theoretical framework allows for this epistemological possibility, wrote on the potential fixity of certain concepts when he elaborates on the non-dialectical nature of ideas of pure reason. Kant is very clear:

> The ideas of pure reason can never be in themselves dialectical; rather, their mere misuse alone must bring it about that there arises from them a deceptive illusion for us. For they are assigned to us by the nature of our

> reason, and this highest tribunal of all rights and claims of our speculation cannot possibly itself contain original delusions and deceptions.[15]

The organizing principles of the subject's experience are the only *a priori* knowledge. This is because it is only those conceptions that are necessary for the very possibility of experience that may be admitted as being *a priori*. Justice, being unnecessary for the very possibility of experience (we can easily imagine an experience without any conception of justice, or wherein a situation referencing justice never arises), is likely not knowledge *a priori*. Reason renders experience sensible, thus allowing the subject to function within a given context. What the idea of justice represents to the individual is a synthesis of the individual's expectations for the world with their desires and needs. Kant's objects of pure reason become the basis for modes of action, they structure the possibility of experiences to which the subject responds and form the basis of her judgments. Perhaps what outrages the rebel most is his ability to identify the misuse of rationality when the subject is objectified into a means for an exterior end. Further, it is the violation of the autonomous use of their reason that riles the rebel into act of negation.

But these acts of negation, as we have said above, are implicit acts of affirmation. A primordinal "This, not that!" issuing from the desire to block the appropriation of subjectivity by the coercive power structures that would enforce a certain harmony. Thus, the postulation of the subject, of the I, is not *necessary*, at least not in Hume's sense. This is precisely because the subject is constantly negotiating a redefinition of what subjectivity means. It is not always the same subjectivity—rather, the necessity is one of a constantly renewed subjectivity; a new subjectivity that comes becomes new again and again through its radical alterity.[16] Thus never identical in terms of sameness, the only necessary postulation is one of some other possibility for being.

Thus the necessary illusion advocated by Hume is refuted. However, this is also the ultimate undoing of the reductionist's arguments.

Kant can claim that these *a priori* objects of knowledge are worthy of confidence because it is they that make experience possible in the first. If the organizing principles of experience are shown to be in any sense reliable, then their basis must be reflective of some basic truth that is justifiable in terms of reason. The same organizing principles that make experience possible form the basis of our judgments. Thus, the rebel sees rationality misused when the subject is made into an object and utilized in a totalized scheme.

If we return to Parfit's conception of personal identity, it would hold that a version of the Principle of Respect for Autonomy would alleviate the violation of objectification by allowing individuals to become an end unto themselves, thereby freeing their will to act autonomously in the generation of their continuity. But this means that the reductionist cannot say that the individual at t_1 is strictly identical with herself at t_2 along any rigid criterion, or delineated by the "right kind of cause"; the word "right" here already introducing a moral element, that one must not develop their identity along certain criteria that would have the "wrong" kinds of causes. The individual is then, from t_1 to t_2, radically *other* to themselves. It is only by the unity of perception brought about by the singular will that makes these others identical with one another. We may speak objectively of continuity, but we speak of a continuity that is objectively determined by the subject's will. Emancipated from the intrusion, the individual cognizes a physical component to herself, permitting the acceptance of others like herself—others always other. The object of the other no longer presents an epistemic problem.

This freedom is the result of Kant's moral philosophy carried to its logical conclusion. The limits of reason define the violation of reason, continually returning to what perception admits to experience. The manifestation of the subject requires that a system function under a unity whose limits are existentially determined to render each part essential and necessary, thus excluding superfluous or incoherent additions. Appropriately, it is Camus' rebel who, "is consummated and perpetuated in the act of real creation, not in criticism or commentary."[17]

The expectation of finding justice in the world resulted in the formation of a concept of justice in dialectical opposition to the injustice perceived in the world instead of deconstructing that injustice to create a new conception. The absolute right that has been take from the subject is essentially the right to creation.

Creation itself follows a limit set within the possibilities of experience. The limit of humanity begins to manifest itself when the individual considers what it is they *ought* to do. This *ought* introduces us into an examination of those relationships that define our experience, among these the most basic and most ancient interpersonal relations. What *ought* to be done is a matter of practicality and is the end toward which reason works its synthesizing operations. When the *ought* becomes a matter of practical consideration, that is, when we consider what we ought to do in order that it be done, we see through Hume's illusion to the seat of our own creation. Therefore, the question of "who am I?" has led to the subsequent question, "What should I do?"

The rejection of an objectifying value system leads beyond a reductionist view of personal identity, freeing the individual from violation of necessitating that a false identity be imposed upon the self. The absolute right is a right to creation, also called autonomy, the self-determination of value, though one that avoids relativism by the appeal to the universality of the ground of the possibility of experience. The disappearance of the "further fact," replaced by the relation "self-as-other," opens upon new responsibilities.

When an exterior value was imposed upon Camus' rebel, exteriority was rejected in a confused appeal to absolute right. The appeal to right could not free a person from subjugation so long as he exists as an object within a power relation. The rebel does not appeal to a right for himself that has not been fulfilled; he is professing a right that transcends individuality and extends to all people. Though consent is never implied within power relations, the relation nevertheless constitutes reciprocation between two parties acting, not on a person as on an object, but on the objective actions committed by persons in order to regulate the possible consequences of those actions. The goal becomes to create a framework for feasible action. It is the reciprocal creation of experience together with the plural demand for autonomy that reveals the self as other and weighs the self with responsibility toward the others. The subject exists within the relation "I am because we are."

And so the individual is faced with the task of reconciling themselves to the world and to those who would objectify her. Through the rejection of exterior values, the possibility of the creation of new value empowers the subject with autonomy. And so the question of ethics returns to be answered. Our absolute right is that autonomy, which amounts to the free creation of our lives according to our own will. This creative act is negotiated, forms an economy with ourselves as with the other, as our self is other when it is self-conscious. The profound immanence of the other is both our right and our responsibility. It sets the horizon of our actions against annihilation, confusing the line between egoism and altruism. The task of the ethical character is not reconciliation with the other. It is the preservation of the otherness of the other qua cognizance of the other that is ourselves. Thus the perennial nature of philosophy's call to "know thyself." Such knowledge constitutes the epistemic component of ethics and alleviates us of any doubt concerning the possible veracity of our moral claims. Our only fear is also our greatest hope—that we have the courage to be our own legislators and the wisdom to judge without illusion.

Notes to Ethics in Rebellion

[1] Albert Camus, *The Rebel*, trans. Anthony Bower, (New York: Random House, 1991), 23.
[2] Foucault, "The Subject and Power." *The Essential Foucault: Selections from the Essential Works of Foucault, 1954-1984*. Ed. Paul Rabinow & Nikolas Rose, (New York: The New Press, 2003), 126.
[3] Ibid. 130
[4] Ibid. 134.
[5] *The Rebel*, 20, 23, 105, and 253 respectively.
[6] Nietzsche, *Genealogy of Morals*. (Mineola: Dover, 2003), 12.
[7] Parfit, *Reasons and Persons*, (New York: Oxford University Press, 1987), 237.
[8] Ibid. 275.
[9] Searle, *Mind: A Brief Introduction*, (New York: Oxford University Press, 2004), 192.
[10] Camus, *Rebel*, 106.
[11] *The Republic of Plato*, trans. Allan Bloom, (New York: The Perseus Book Group, 1991), 198.
[12] Ibid. 189.
[13] Ibid.
[14] Camus, *Rebel*, 13.
[15] Kant, *The Critique of Pure Reason*, trans. Werner Pluhar, (Indianapolis: Hackett Publishing, 1996), 638.
[16] Two essays in the current volume reflect this position, "The Ontological I," and also, "On the Freedom of Action." A rigorous account of the subjects radical alterity can be found in these essays.
[17] Camus, *Rebel*, 272.

NIHILISM AND ARCHETYPE; TRAGEDY IN *BLACK SWAN*

The totality of *Black Swan* is revealed in the film's opening shot. The entirety if the film is contained in this image and the plot follows logically from it to the consummatory end.

As the film opens, we see a ballerina, her arched back to an audience advantageously situated upstage of the figure, insinuating the viewer into the performance, placing our vantage on stage with her. A spotlight illuminates the ballerina. Thus backlit, the ballerina is encased in her frail periphery. The lace of the tutu, the white porcelain patina of her skin radiates the virginal aura of the white swan. Delicate, demur, brilliantly aloof, withdrawing from her lover at the moment she entices him nearer to her. But the spotlight reveals the contradiction in her presentation.

The softness of her peripheral frame encompasses the hard truth of her body whose opaque center allows no light to penetrate it. The black core of the swan pushes forth a demur façade in order to conceal the destructive element that, for all her apparent innocence, is inherent within the virgin archetype. For what is virginity if not something to be lost, something to which growing up amounts to a process of losing, of getting lost—the loss faith, of innocence and, perhaps, even of ourselves.

Nina is this becoming lost. *Black Swan* is the story of her sacrifice to the archetype and of her transcendence of the archetype in a synthesis of opposites, in the reconciliation of contradictions. Ultimately, the consummation is death, and a greater death than the 'little death' of the orgasm. It is annihilation.

This annihilation is the consequence of an aesthetic of perfection.

Since the plot of the movie involves a new interpretation of *Swan Lake* with the same dancer in the roles of both the white and black swans, it makes sense to view the film's genre as a new interpretation of Greek tragedy. The tragic heroine is characterized by seriousness and dignity, yet her greatness is not undermined by some mistake, as in classical Hellenic tragedy. Rather, the heroine is thoroughly nihilistic, purposefully sacrificing herself to the art of perfection, murdering herself, not committing suicide, but allowing her dual nature to run its logical course.

Further, Nina's tragic irony is complicated by her split personality. Traditionally, a character that is tragically ironic is so because they are ignorant of making a grave mistake while everyone around them knows fully that the tragic protagonist is fated for catastrophe. Everyone in the audience is aware of the impending downfall while the character remains ignorant, striving to the very end to divert what is ultimately inevitable.

Nina is her own mistake. She has constructed her own austerity so completely that *any* situation that sexualizes her is immediately a violation. There is a scene shortly after Nina is awarded the lead in *Swan Lake* where Thomas Leroy, the prestigious director of the ambitious new production, seduces her in order to demonstrate how the Black Swan character should be danced. Thomas' actions are wildly inappropriate, even if the lesson Nina takes from them are appropriate for her role as the Black Swan. But how could they not be inappropriate? Nina must violate herself in order to reach the blackness within her crystalline shell.

"That was me seducing you," Thomas says. "It needs to be the other way around."

Thomas does not consummate his seduction. He doesn't even get under Nina's clothes, but his lesson does get under her skin, and Nina is soon digging beneath her epidermis in order to uncover the black swan within—literally. She scratches herself, cuts her nails until they bleed, and is unable to follow through with several attempts to masturbate (in one attempt she becomes highly aroused only to discover her mother is asleep in a nearby chair—a fact which derails her ecstasy).

Yet she seems to be aware of these things about herself. She is not ignorant of her actions, in the way that Œdipus his ignorant of his actions. She sees the damage she is doing to herself and works to conceal it from the others who can only see the presentation, the demur virgin that is, as Thomas says again and again, "frigid."

In *Black Swan*, the tragedy is internalized. Nina may know *that* she does these things, she knows what she does, but she cannot come to terms with *why* she does them. Her frigidity keeps Thomas out, but it encases her within herself as well, and provides a barrier against which she herself must struggle. This tension between the being imprisoned in oneself (descendent from the Greek *soma-*) and attempting to be free of, to transcend, the corporal prison (as Socrates insists *psuche* is capable) is the catalyst to Nina's dissolution.

Her freedom is destruction. She destroys the cloister of youth constructed by her mother. Yet, Nina's mother does not victimize her the way Carrie's mother victimized Carrie in Stephen King's comparatively flat narrative. Nina is, above all, *successful*, and successful in ways her mother was not. We get that her mother "gave up" her career due to being pregnant with Nina. However, Nina makes it clear that she views her mother's career as having been at an end regardless of the pregnancy. The life of a ballerina is short, thus the tremendous pressure Nina places on herself to land the role of the Swans.

Just as Nina destroys the past represented by her mother's cloistered apartment, she destroys her future as well. There is a natural tension between Nina and Beth, the prima ballerina which Nina is to replace in the company. But Beth is Nina's future. Here is her end, which much also be destroyed. Though Beth has failed in attempting suicide, Nina will not allow herself this same failure. When she lashes out at Beth in the hospital, it is Beth as Nina that is attacked; it is Nina's renunciation of her own short career. What better way to overcome this end than by controlling it and ending in an act of consummate beauty?

Nina is fractured, identifying parts of herself with those around her, allowing these personifications to feed her ego and elaborate her fantasies. When she finally has an orgasm, it's during a hallucinated lesbian tryst with Lily who is Nina's only serious competition. This imagined sexual conquest is at once the conquest of Lily who serves as the vehicle of Nina's satisfaction and at the same time is Nina's own conquest of herself—depicted as the metamorphosis of Lily into Nina and back again. Thus the sexualized Nina is someone else. During this encounter, Nina's mother is locked out of Nina's room, the barrier is up and Nina is within herself, alienating herself through the assumption of Lily's more liberated sexual persona.

The problematic of the film is that all of these are personas. They are contradictory masks that Nina commands herself to master. But this mastery comes at the price of her sanity.

It is only the perfect unity of the fractured personas within the presentation of Nina's performance that reveals her fate and the authenticity of her Self as the Black/White Swan. We began on stage with the performer, and we end on stage with her. And she has brought the audience into her perfection as well, turning the tragic tables completely, inverting the tragic irony so that now, in her perfection, she is the sole heiress of the madness of her perfection. It is now the audience and chorus that is ignorant and the Swan Princess sails above them and assails them with her irreproachable virginity, cast aside in the instant of the Black Swans birth, only to return wounded and bleeding (an appropriate symbolic) to die the vestal death of her snow white archetype.

Nina is many people and no one. She is pure presentation in the Schopenhauerian sense, and the veil of the phenomenal is drawn back to reveal a horror beneath: the horror of nihilism, of masochism, of self-defeat. Her annihilation serves as the final virgin sacrifice that realizes the aesthetic archetype whose mask she wears, not only on stage, but throughout the film. For all her depth and beauty, Nina is a hollow character, a hollow character whose own density results in her implosion, the collapse that tragedy presents as the world's great beauty.

We may cry, or find it absurd, but like Sisyphus, one must imagine Nina happy.

THE FREE SPIRIT PARALLAX

1. *The Free Spirit*—The Free Spirit must appear to us as a paradox. In the classical sense, in the sense that Plato or Descartes would be accustomed to, the Spirit is that subliminally free essence that *is*, a transcendent Being that overcomes Becoming. But Spirit cannot be free because it is bound to the flesh and bones of mortal men who are and were. It is not only the limitation of extension, the problems of entropy that arise in the physical; it is the temporal nature of Becoming that thwarts the sublime freedom of the Spirit. Temporality contextualizes the spirit into a subjectivity that becomes and reveals itself, ultimately, as a totality.

Again bounded, the spirit finds itself enclosed on all sides by space, time, and finally by language through which it finds expression. Here symbology comes to our aid. Language, as signs and symbols, can reveal what is pertinent to our concerns. Nietzsche's discussion of the Free Spirit allows us a rich system of symbols with which to realize the concept of the Free Spirit. Yet in Nietzsche too, the Free Spirit comes as a paradox. It is this symbolism of paradox that is to be explored. Although paradox arises in much older articulations of Spirit and also of freedom it is Nietzsche who allows paradox and contradiction into his formulation of the Free Spirit and sets us up for the struggle between freedom and determination, a struggle that has occupied contemporary metaphysics for sometime.

The preoccupation with this tension is in folly. As I shall show, the contradiction present in the concept of the Free Spirit is irreconcilable and necessary. The struggle is not a struggle that is to be concluded. There is no winner in the conflict of determination and freedom. It is from the conflict itself that our understanding of freedom arises and from our own will to freedom that our understanding of determinism arises. The paradox is a complementary one that offers us choice, chance, and a sense of ourselves.

2. *The Conflict*—"The term 'free spirit' here is not to be understood in any other sense; it means a spirit that has *become* free, that has again taken possession of itself."[1] This Nietzsche writes in reference to the subtitle of his book *Human, All Too Human*. But what Nietzsche was driving at in *Ecce Homo* appears earlier in his works and these earlier passages are a key to understanding why it is that *Human, All Too Human* is a "book for free spirits." In an essay titled "On the Uses and Disadvantages of History for Life," Nietzsche examines the role of history in human existence and how the past figures into plotting the course of the future. The germ of conflict rests in these uses and disadvantages of history because we

must confront our history in order to move beyond it. And then, moving beyond it, the confrontation becomes past and must be again confronted. We get ahead of ourselves, and so perhaps a look at how Nietzsche viewed history. To understand his view, we must consider both memory and forgetting.

"Thus: it is possible," Nietzsche writes, "to live almost without memory…but it is altogether impossible to *live* at all without forgetting."[2] Why must we forget in order to live while memory appears *dangerous* to life? The answer comes in the next breath. Nietzsche emphasizes, "*there is a degree of sleeplessness, of rumination, of the historical sense, which is harmful and ultimately fatal to the living thing, whether this living thing be a man or a people or a culture.*"[3] The conflict is given here in historical terms. It is very clear that the unhistorical is the base from which anything human must grow, but that an excess of history will destroy just as the construction of the historical was a process of creation.[4] Is this historical conflict the only conflict though? It seems to lack something that ties history to freedom and to the notion of the free spirit. Where else rings of conflict?

"Even if *language*, here as elsewhere, will not get over its awkwardness, and will continue to talk of opposites where there are only degrees and many subtleties of gradation," writes Nietzsche in the second part of *Beyond Good & Evil*.[5] Language itself is conflicted and engaged in a discussion of opposites and contradictions. Nietzsche sees language as conflicted within itself, pointing as he does to gradation and subtlety. The problem here lies in the Being of language, that is, in the fact that language objectifies and crystallizes the things it signifies in the process of defining it. By fixing a word to an object, the object becomes static and so becomes nothing other than what it is. The word is intended for a static object and misses because the object is in transit between two states of being. Confusion and ambiguity come into play in the discourse. It enters when the discourse involves only determinism and free will.

Between these two extremes whose mutual exclusivity puts them at an infinite distance from one another lays an insurmountable dilemma. It is in this infinite gulf that the true conflict of the free spirit reveals itself. The discourse has allowed us a choice of either/or: either freedom or determinism. One cannot be reconciled with the other without loosing a sense of itself, so the definitions imply. Where then, is the free spirit? What was its choice? Clearly, the obvious answer seems to be that the free spirit chose its freedom. But what if it chose determinism and by choosing its own determination for itself was thereby liberated?

3. *Involving Subjectivity in Symbolism*—Let us not confuse ourselves and assume that the free spirit is an abstract concept that cannot be articulated in everyday language or whose being lies in antiquated academic writings. No, we must own up to the fact that the free spirit is among us if it is not we ourselves. Am I a free spirit? This is the question of the hour, or perhaps the question of all time, and if that is so then we must ask ourselves "how are we to answer the conflict?" It has been suggested that a distinction can be made within Nietzsche's work between the causal condition of subjectivity and whether or not it is possible to attribute to the features of

subjectivity a control over the movements of said subjectivity.[6] I believe this is a useful distinction to draw. First, it allows us to consider the possibility that a free being may be constituted of essentially "unfree" components, but there are deeper implications.

What I had in mind when seconding this suggestion is a return to the conflict ourselves, not a return to the analysis of the conflict as such, but a real return to the conflict in itself and so to the conflict within ourselves. When we involve subjectivity we involve ourselves. And so, we must address this strange symbolism with which we've been involved. The symbolism, naturally, is one of conflict and of choice. We must choose among these symbols and one of the choices is a means to our freedom.

There must then be choices that lead to our not being free and these Nietzsche is quick to identify. The decadent, for one, symbolizes reactive unfreedom for Nietzsche.[7] The most woeful type of decadent is one exhibiting the condition of disgregation. Dudley explains,

> …one suffering from disgregation does not have a will that integrates her disparate instincts into a larger whole, apart from which those instincts have no function and are not exercised, but instead is merely a composite, an aggregate of instincts and drives whose expression us not organized by any larger purpose.[8]

The whole conception smacks of deterministic factors that control a person entirely. Included are desires and instincts of the person himself that are not under the supervision of the Will in one way or another. The game at this point is falling along standard lines that are easy to explicate. But does Nietzsche ever leave us there? In short, no, he does not. So why focus on the decadent?

In part, it is to show what freedom is *not* so that we may know what it *is*. Then again, we could just as easily show what freedom *is* in order to know what it is *not*. I think this course we have taken is the sensible one because of the challenge issued by Nietzsche himself, a challenge that, for the decadent, is a condemnation. Dudley points to the repetition of this challenge, once in *Richard Wagner in Bayreuth*, and once in *The Gay Science*.[9] Nietzsche writes,

> ...the free man can be good or evil but the unfree man is a disgrace to nature...he who wants to become free has to become so through his own actions and that freedom falls into no one's lap like a miraculous gift.[10]

Again, the language of becoming figures heavily in Nietzsche's thought. But no real support for the notion Dudley utilizes of a "larger purpose." Becoming free through one's own actions implies no larger purpose per se. The assertion only makes sense if the larger purpose is in some significant way only a phrase to indicate ourselves. That is, only within ourselves can the larger purpose be cultivated. Further, it is by our hand that cultivation occurs. We return to the conflicted subjectivity.

Certain commentators, Mike W. Martin for example, will focus on "purposefully-generated" institutions and practices.[11] I think this is in line with Dudley's basic concern with a "larger purpose" which provides the context for freedom. That said it also falls into the same folly. It seems noble to avoid "Sartrian subjectivism and Nietzschean egoism" in the context of moral creativity, for the sake of defending the weak I suppose.[12] But how much of Nietzsche can be avoided before we are no longer discussing Nietzsche, and possibly, are no longer discussing moral creativity? For instance, if the moral choice is always couched in institutions, or if Good lives are necessarily both "personally satisfying and morally acceptable," as John Kekes put it for Martin, then there is really no creativity involved except in the finding of new ways to uphold old moral values.[13] Such are certainly not Nietzschean attitudes. Maybe it is decadence. It is decadence driven by the instinct to bolster morality and save it from itself.

It is best if these commentators forget this notion of "larger purpose" and "purposefully-generated" and remember instead they deal with symbols. How can anything free, in the Nietzschean sense of free, not be purposeful? The free spirit, from where the discussion has lead us so far, appears full of purpose, full of its own purpose and generated by it. How can it be, even for the decadent, that we generate anything without purpose? Even generating without a purpose would seem to generate with the purpose of purposelessness. And so, like the return to subjectivity, we return to paradox. So much have we gotten from the involvement of subjectivity in the discourse, and alas! with subjectivity we have involved ourselves.

4. *Acceptance*—This conflict must be embraced as primordinal lest we destroy ourselves in its resolution.

5. *The Struggle to Freedom*—Commenting on Freud's decision to stay away from the study of Nietzsche, Charles Bingham writes, "Doesn't the decision to stay away from Nietzsche's thought already imply that he [Freud] actually read Nietzsche, and that he *does* remember what he has read?"[14] There is a sense in which Freud struggles to be free of Nietzsche as an educator when he said that he "rejected the study of Nietzsche although—no, because—it was plain that I would find insights in him very similar to psychoanalytic ones."[15] Freud is not alone in the struggle as he sees it, against his 'teacher.' Nietzsche himself devotes much ink to this precise topic and very deliberately involves the language of memory and forgetting into his discussion of the theme. Memory cannot stand alone of course; it needs its counterpart forgetting in order to hold as a defining aspect of the human condition.[16]

In one sense, it is our memory that we struggle against in our attempts to be free. It is memory that binds us to our culture by the remembrance of it. Not only the mere remembrance binds us but also the memory of its supposed importance to us. The prejudices we hold are tied intimately to this fact. That we hold these prejudices as truth, or as an approximation of truth even, does not help us in our struggle to be free for, as Nietzsche indicates, we need be willing to question even these "truths."[17] In questioning these alleged truths we will ultimately indict the whole because "truths" are not born in a vacuum but instead grow together in a web of meanings and implications.[18] So arises the system of symbols that has become our concern here. And, again, we are implicated in these symbols often.

It is the case that the symbols used to articulate not only our prejudices but also our desire to be free of these prejudices are inextricable from the system in which these symbols developed. It may be the case that we create new values and new symbols, but these new creations must stand in reference to the historical symbolism from which they digress. The affirmation of a new value implies the rejection of an old value that stands in judgment.[19] The theme of this affirmation/rejection relationship runs throughout Camus' analysis of rebellion, during which he comments extensively on Nietzsche's philosophy. The point is well taken and well put.

So are we ever really free then? If we must stand in relation to the past, then the past is always definitive of us at least in some sense. But does this significantly undermine our possible freedom? I do not believe it does and I don't believe Nietzsche took it to either. Part of the struggle's importance lies in the struggle itself, not in its resolution. I hold that a process, not of resolution, but of conflict and contradiction is the key to understanding the free spirit. The free spirit is a symbol of this contradiction we feel between history and tradition on one hand, and our will to power on the other. I use Nietzsche's phrase lightly here. The "will to power" is a way for me to express the intentional movement of a person toward not only that which she desires, but toward a fulfillment of herself, of motivations that are attributable to her. Unfortunately, the scope of this essay does not admit an in depth or remotely complete discussion of intentionality or the will.[20] However, we may enter into a discussion of these subjects that will suffice for our understanding of the symbolism involved in the free spirit and how these forces play into its actualization.

6. *Beyond Acceptance*—Once the conflict within ourselves has been accepted as primordinal the movement must be made beyond the simplicity of accepting the conflict. Nietzsche has given us the tools to progress in this movement though we must be bold enough to make the step ourselves and so be closer to understanding the free spirit and what it entails. What would it mean to be beyond acceptance?

Mere acceptance appears as a sign of passivity. To accept the conflict we must simply allow it to occur. There need be no fight toward resolution, or an activity involving the end of conflict. Being active in the conflict is the first move beyond mere acceptance. The involvement of subjectivity again plays a central role in the development of this interplay between the conflicted and what conflicts. Indeed, it seems that what is desirable in place of the resolution of conflict is the proliferation of conflict. At first this appears illogical, or at least undesirable. But if we consider some Nietzschean advice there may be a way in which the course of most resistance as it were can be the most fruitful course. "Is it any wonder that we should become suspicious," Nietzsche wrote, "lose patience, and turn away impatiently?...Suppose we want truth: *why not rather* untruth? And uncertainty? Even ignorance?"[21] In short, we need question the very value of truth, it's meaning. These precepts are derived from the conflict we feel.

It is history that burdens us with meaning and with the prejudices of philosophers who have always been concerned with truth and its attainment. The stance taken toward history is the key to understanding the development of a free spirit. It is no surprise that Nietzsche follows the section in *Beyond Good & Evil* called "The Prejudices of Philosophers" with his section on the "Free Spirit." The two concepts are inextricably bound to one another. To be free the prejudices of philosophers must be overcome. But not just those of philosophers, it is our own prejudices as well that must be overcome. This is a process and is perhaps never complete. I must stress here that Nietzsche was using the term "prejudice" in a different context than we use the word today where it takes on a very particular meaning and is involved largely in the symbols of racism and intolerance. For Nietzsche's philosophy a prejudice is simply a pre-judgment, one that goes unanalyzed and informs our interpretation of the world with our acting on our own accord. To simply follow a prejudice is to be unaware of a certain kind of ignorance. This particular ignorance is an ignorance of the openness of history. In following a prejudice there is an implicit assumption that the past is interpreted in this one certain way and that is the generally correct way and so there is no reason or no imperative to look at history any other way and thus derive different mode of actions from the new perspective.

Enter forgetfulness. We must forget prejudice in one sense. However, it is crucial also to remember prejudice in order to avoid falling into the trap of prejudicial blindness. Contradiction appears in this suggestion: to remember what we must forget. But it is a useful contradiction, perhaps the most useful to our endeavor. To resolve this contradiction would be to thwart the struggle toward freedom. To be free, the struggle must remain and be ongoing. We must be conflicted in order to be presented with a choice. The choice cannot subside or our freedom dissolves back into prejudice.

I am aware that these claims clash with and occasionally anger philosophers who quest always for resolution into neat and tidy systems of logical relations. But even logic has counterparts, and not merely in the illogical. To understand logic we have a sense of the illogical, but also of the non-logical, what has no relation to logic. Is this possible? Well, I have to admit it depends on the perspective taken. The prejudices of philosophers will tell us that the logical is inextricable from thought. But perhaps the poet will tell something different, and the painter again may speak of the power of the emotions. And what will the poor speak of? Or the rich? The black man and the white man and the women of these groups and women in general or a communist or Communist or fascist? What does democracy say, if it could speak, for it seems it is really we who speak for it and through it once the prejudices of each of these "isms" are adopted as our own. The philosopher may say there must be one ultimate perspective that is the objective one. Find it and show it to me and I will believe it.

7. *Impossible*—Impossible I say. The objectivity shown to me is nothing but the subjective expression of some objectivity that I cannot access. Subjective objectivity is still subjective and so again

the return to subjectivity as if it would recur eternally, but alas, subjectivity must die.

8. *Eternal Conflict, not Infinite*—When I speak of eternally recurring subjectivity or conflict, for I believe I have demonstrated how subjectivity is symbolic of conflict (hence the avoidance or outright condemnation of subjectivity by philosophers of the past), please do not mistake me to mean infinite. By eternal, I mean to indicate a weight that is born. It is the weight of the conflict we are faced with, but also the weight of the choice presented to us within the conflict. The choice is unavoidable and the eternal recurrence is a metaphor for the ultimate responsibility imposed on us by the choosing. Nietzsche comments,

> the ideal of the most high-spirited, alive, and world-affirming human being who has not only come to terms and learned to get along with whatever was and is, but who wants to have *what was and is* repeated into all eternity, shouting insatiably *da capo*—not only to himself but to the whole play and spectacle…at bottom to him who needs precisely this spectacle…who makes it necessary because again and again he needs himself—and makes himself necessary—What? And this wouldn't be—*circulus vitiosus deus*?[22]

What a curious phrase Nietzsche has left us with here. Walter Kaufmann ponders over the meaning of this last phrase "*circulus vitiosus deus*" in a footnote that suggests three meanings: 1) A vicious circle made god, 2) God is a vicious circle, or 3) the circle is a vicious god.[23] I must insist that it is all three and also chide Kaufmann for including a question mark at the end of these three suggestions. It is clear from the context that the question mark belongs to Nietzsche's own statement "And this wouldn't be..." and not exclusively to the phrase *"circulus vitiosus deus"* which need not necessarily be a question itself. The question is whether or not this longed for recurrence is *circulus vitiosus deus*. But how can the meaning be threefold?

For one, it is interpretive. Nietzsche, being an astute philologist, was most likely aware of the ambiguity of this phrase. An interesting observation: if the vicious circle is God, and God is dead, then the vicious circle is itself dead. It is dead the moment it is crystallized into symbols, thus terminating its movement around again. But the Free Spirit endures the movement and finds itself coming around again; for the Free Spirit, the vicious circle is not God. Perhaps the circle is a vicious god. Kaufmann believed this to be the least likely interpretation.[24] Unless there is some nuance of Latin that I'm missing I don't see why this interpretation is particularly less likely than the others. Why more than "a vicious circle made god"? All options employ similar notions and join together under the immense weight of the affirmation made by the "highest spirit."

The choice of this spirit is an eternal choice, one that must be faced again and again and again. It is the recurring opposition of subjectivity to the history that determines it and in determining it, sets it against itself in the struggle for freedom. When we speak of the viciousness of circularity, it is in reference to an argument whose circularity, for lack of better words, proves the argument wrong. The Free Spirit must always be proving itself wrong in order to be free. This is the disavowal of prejudice, this is the indictment of moral judgment, and this is the open interpretation of history. For the Free Spirit, this circle cannot end unless it surrenders finally to the weigh it could not bear. But if it bears the weight, like Sisyphus it finds happiness in its labor because in its labor it is defining itself and, like Sisyphus, its labor is eternal. It must be this contradiction for all that it is until the end of its being, no, until the end of its becoming, until its death.

9. *The Circle Closed*—We have come to an end. Symbols abound and indicate one another and become convoluted and ambiguous. Above all things I cannot be clear about that which is admittedly unclear. I must admit complications and contradictions. I must be free with my words. Does this make me a Free Spirit? Too bold, too hasty.

Of what value is it to me to assert my freedom? It would be enough to question, like the Sphinx, to find the value of questions. I think that the Free Spirit must forget his freedom in order to maintain it. In forgetting, each time he comes to conflict he remembers again and is capable of asserting the most dreadful choice, the choice that hovers over him always, the choice of prejudice or revaluation. I have shown the value of these contradictions. Though it is to the chagrin of the philosophical tradition, I am not alone in my affirmation of conflict and ambiguity.

I have read, "This recourse to the archaic, the nocturnal, and the oneiric, which is also an approach to the birthplace of language, represents an attempt to avoid the difficulties in the problem of a starting point in philosophy."[25] The author, Paul Ricoeur, a few lines later also asserts, "a meditation on symbols starts from the fullness of language"[26] and I have found that to be the case here. Wherever we start in this discourse, we come to the Free Spirit with a multitude of baggage. It is within the symbol of the Free Spirit that the baggage conflicts, as if for space, and overflows its compartments in search of new meanings.

The Free Spirit *can be* ourselves, though it is often no one. We must be able to accept certain troubling concepts and be able to view the problem from a variety of perspectives. On this I can say no more lest I risk eternally returning to the same themes that have proven so central to the issue above and throughout this entire volume of works. Subjectivity, conflict, and interpretation: these themes have informed our discussion and given the Free Spirit an "essence" of sorts. Of course, the essence is dynamic and cannot remain static. The three words I have chosen merely hint at what we each must come to on our own. I cannot explicate the fullness of the Free Spirit no matter how long I go on about it. I find it best to stop and to close the circle. There is no way out of it, just as there is no way in. We find ourselves here, within subjectivity, engaged in the conflicts it manifests, and given easily to interpreting as we see fit. And so, I must insist emphatically, with all of my being—*da capo*!

1. *The Free Spirit*—…

Notes to The Free Spirit Parallax

[1] Nietzsche, Friedrich, "Ecce Homo," *Basic Writings of Nietzsche*, Trans. Walter Kaufmann, (New York: Random House, 2000), 739.
[2] Nietzsche, Friedrich, "On the uses and advantages of history to life," *Untimely Meditations*, Trans. R. J. Hollingdale, (New York: Cambridge University Press, 2007), 62.
[3] Ibid., 62.
[4] Ibid., 64.
[5] Nietzsche, Friedrich, "Beyond Good & Evil," *Basic Writings of Nietzsche*, Trans. Walter Kaufmann, (New York: Random House, 2000), 225.
[6] Guay, Robert, "The 'I's Have it: Nietzsche on Subjectivity," *Inquiry 49.3* (June 2006): 221.
[7] Dudley, Will, "Freedom in and Through Nietzsche's Tragic Genealogy," *International Studies in Philosophy 37:3* (2005): 128.
[8] Ibid., 128.
[9] Ibid, 127.
[10] Nietzsche, Friedrich, "Richard Wagner in Bayreuth," *Untimely Meditations*, Trans. R. J. Hollingdale, (New York: Cambridge University Press, 2007), 252.
[11] Martin, Mike W., "Moral Creativity," *International Journal of Applied Philosophy* 20:1 (2006), 56.
[12] Ibid., 55.
[13] Ibid., 64.
[14] Bingham, Charles, "Montaigne, Nietzsche, and the Mnemotechnics of Student Agency," *Educational Philosophy and Theory* 39:2 (January 2007): 169.
[15] Gay, Peter, *Freud, A Life in Our Time* (New York: Anchor Books, 1988), 46.
[16] Bingham, Charles, "Montaigne, Nietzsche, and the Mnemothechnics of Student Agency," 169.
[17] Nietzsche, Friedrich, *Beyond Good & Evil*, 199.
[18] Ibid., 217.
[19] Camus, Albert, *The Rebel*, Trans. Justin O'Brian, (New York: RandomHouse, 1991), 13.

[20] A more robust discussion of the themes of intentionality and the Will are found in my essay "On the Freedom of Action," contained in the present volume.
[21] Nietzsche, Friedrich, *Beyond Good & Evil*, 199.
[22] Ibid., 258.
[23] Kaufmann, Walter, "Note 17 to *Beyond Good & Evil* Part 3," *Basic Writings of Nietzsche*, (New York: Random House, 2000), 258.
[24] Ibid., 258.
[25] Ricoeur, Paul, "The Hermeneutics of Symbols and Philosophical Reflection: I," Trans. Denis Savage, *The Conflict of Interpretation*, (Evanston: Northwestern University Press, 1996), 287.
[26] Ibid., 287.

BIBLIOGRAPHY

Arendt, Hannah. *Between Past and Future: Eight Exercises in Political Thought*. New York: Penguin Books, 1977.

Aristotle. *The Complete Works, vol. 1 Princeton/Bollingen Series LXXI: 2*. ed. Jonathan Barnes. Princeton, NJ: Princeton University Press, 1984.

-- *The Complete Works, vol. 2 Princeton/Bollingen Series LXXI: 2*. ed. Jonathan Barnes. Princeton, NJ: Princeton University Press, 1984.

Aquinas, St. Thomas. *Summa Theologiae*, I, q. 2 a. 3, trans. George Brantl in *Great Religions of Modern Man: Catholicism*. New York: George Braziller, 1962; 30—32

Augustine of Hippo. *The Confessions*. trans. Albert Cook Outler. Mineola, NY: Dover Publications, 2002.

-- *Eighty-Three Different Questions*, trans. David L. Mosher. Washington DC: The Catholic University of America Press, 1982.

-- *On Genesis*, trans. Roland J. Teske, S.J. Washington, DC: The Catholic University of America Press, 1991.

-- *Sermo* XXX-VIII, ii, 3. *Library of the Fathers of the Holy Catholic Church*, eds. E. P. Pusey, J. H. Newman, J. Keble, & C. Merriot. Oxford: J. H. Parker, 1838—85.

Bergson, Henri. *Matter and Memory*. trans. N. M. Paul & W. S. Palmer. New York: Zone Books, 2005.

Berkeley, George. "Principles of Human Knowledge." *The Empiricists*. New York: Anchor Books, 1974; 135—216.

Bingham, Charles. "Montaigne, Nietzsche, and the Mnemotechnics of Student Agency," *Educational Philosophy and Theory* 39:2 (January 2007)

Book of the Dead: The Papyrus of Ani in the British Museum, The. Egyptian text with interlinear transliteration, translation, introduction, and notes by E. A. Wallis Budge. London: Trustees of the British Museum, 1895.

Camus, Albert. *The First Man*. trans. David Hapgood. New York: Vintage International, 1996.

-- *L'homme Révolte*. Paris: Gallimard, 1951.

-- *The Myth of Sisyphus*. trans. Justin O'Brien. New York: Vintage International, 1991.

-- *Notebooks 1942—1951*. trans. Justin O'Brien, New York: Harvest/HBJ, 1978.

-- *The Rebel*. trans. Anthony Bower. New York: Vintage International, 1991.

Chisholm, Roderick. "Human Freedom and the Self." *Agency and Responsibility*, ed. Laura Waddell Ekstrom, (Boulder, CO: Westview Press, 2001); 126—137.

Cohen, Morris & Ernest Nagel. *An Introduction to Logic and Scientific Method*. New York: Harcourt, Brace & World, 1934.

Deleuze, Gilles. *Difference and Repetition*. Trans. Paul Patton. New York: Columbia University Press, 1994.

Dennett, Daniel. *Elbow Room: Varieties of Free Will Worth Having*, (Cambridge MA: The MIT Press, 1984).

-- *Freedom Evolves*, (New York: Penguin Putnam, 2003).

Derrida, Jacques. *Margins of Philosophy*. trans. Alan Bass. Chicago: University of Chicago Press, 1984.

-- *The Politics of Friendship*. trans. George Collins. New York: Verso, 2005.

-- *Writing and Difference*. trans. Alan Bass. Chicago: University of Chicago Press, 1978.

Descartes, René. "Discourse on the Method of Rightly Conducting the Reason and Seeking Truth in the Sciences." *The Rationalists*. trans. John Veitch. New York: Anchor Books, 1974; 39—98.

-- "Meditations on the First Philosophy." *The Rationalists*. trans. John Veitch. New York: Anchor Books, 1974; 99—175.

Dudley, Will. "Freedom in and Through Nietzsche's Tragic Genealogy," *International Studies in Philosophy 37:3* (2005).

Emerson, Ralph Waldo. *The Essential Writings*. Ed. Brooks Atkinson. New York: The Modern Library, 2000.

Foucault, Michel. *The Essential Foucault: Selections from the Essential Works of Foucault, 1954-1984*. Ed. Paul Rabinow & Nikolas Rose, (New York: The New Press, 2003).

Freeman, Kathleen. *Ancilla to the Pre-Socratic Philosophers*. Cambridge: Harvard University Press, 1983.

Freiere, Paulo. *Pedagogy of the Oppressed*. trans. Myra Bergman Ramos, New York: Continuum Press, 1970.

Gadamer, Hans-Georg. *Philosophical Hermeneutics*. trans. David E. Linge. Berkeley, CA: University of California Press, 1977.

-- *Truth and Method* 2nd ed. trans. Joel Weinsheimer & Donald G. Marshall. New York: Continuum Press, 2004.

Gay, Peter. *Freud, A Life in Our Time*. New York: Anchor Books, 1988.

Guay, Robert. "The 'I's Have it: Nietzsche on Subjectivity," *Inquiry 49.3* (June 2006).

Hegel, G. W. F. *Phenomenology of Spirit*. Trans. A.V. Miller. Oxford: Oxford University Press, 1977.

Heidegger, Martin. *Being and Time*. trans. John Macquarrie & Edward Robinson. New York: Harper & Row, 1962.

-- *Parmenides*. trans. André Schuwer & Richard Rojcewicz. Bloomington, Il: Indiana University Press, 1998.

-- *Sein und Zeit*. Tübingen: Max Niemeyer, 1967.

Hillard, Asa G. III, Larry Williams, & Nia Damali eds. *The Teachings of Ptahhotep: The Oldest Book in the World*. Atlanta: Blackwood Press, 1987.

Hord, Fred Lee (Mzee Lasana Okpara) & Jonathan Scott Lee. "'I am because we are': An Introduction to Black Philosophy." *I*

Am Because We Are: Readings in Black Philosophy. Amherst, MA: University of Massachusetts Press, 1995; 1—16.

Hume, David. "An Enquiry Concerning Human Understanding." *The Empiricists*. New York: Anchor Books, 1974; 307—430.

-- *Treatise of Human Nature*. ed. L. A. Shelby-Bigge. Oxford: Clarendon Press, 1896.

Husserl, Edmund. *Logical Investigations vol. 1*. trans. J. N. Findlay. New York: Routledge, 2001.

-- *Logical Investigations vol. 2*. trans. J. N. Findlay. New York: Routledge, 2001.

-- "Phenomenology and Anthropology." Trans. Richard G. Schmitt, *Realism and the Background of Phenomenology*, ed. Roderick Chisholm, Glencoe: The Free Press, 1960;

Irigaray, Luce. "The Question of the Other." trans. Noah Guynn, *Yale French Studies*, no. 87, Another Look, Another Woman: Retranslations of French (1995); 7—19.

-- "What Other Are We Talking About?" trans Esther Marion. *Yale French Studies*, no. 104, Encounters with Levinas (2004); 67—81.

James, William. *The Essential Writings*. Ed. Bruce W. Wilshire. Albany, NY: SUNY Press, 1984.

Kane, Robert. "Responsibility, Luck and Chance: Reflections on Free Will and Indeterminism." *Agency and Responsibility*, ed. Laura Waddell Ekstrom, (Boulder, CO: Westview Press, 2001).

Kant, Immanuel. *Critique of Pure Reason*. trans. Norman Kemp Smith. New York: Palgrave Macmillan, 2007.

-- *Critique of Pure Reason*. trans. Werner Pluhar. Indianapolis: Hackett, 1996.

-- *Logic*. trans. Robert S. Hartman & Wolfgang Schwarz. New York: Dover Publications, Inc. 1988.

Korgaard, Christine M. "Personal Identity and the Unity of Agency: A Kantian Response to Parfit." *Philosophy and Public Affairs* 18:2 (1989); 109—23.

Koyré, Alexandre. "Hegel á Iena." *Etudes d'histoire de la pensée philosophique*. Paris: Armand Colin, 1961

Lacan, Jacques. "The mirror stage." *Identity: a reader*. eds. Paul du Gay, Jessica Evans, & Peter Redman. London: SAGE Publishing, 2000; 44—50.

Leibniz, Gottfried Wilhelm. "Discourse on Metaphysics." *The Rationalists*. trans. George Montgomery & rev. Albert R. Chandler. New York: Anchor Books, 1974; 409—54.

-- *Early Mathematical Manuscripts*. trans. J. M. Child. Derby, England: Merchant Books, 1919.

-- "The Monadology." *The Rationalists*. trans. George Montgomery & rev. Albert R. Chandler. New York: Anchor Books, 1974; 455—71.

Levinas, Emmanuel. *Entre Nous: Thinking-of-the-other*. Trans. Michael B. Smith & Barbara Harshav. New York: Continuum Press, 2006.

-- *Of God Who Comes to Mind*. trans. Bettina Bergo. Stanford, CA: Stanford University Press, 1998.

-- *Otherwise Than Being*. trans. Alphonso Lingis. Pittsburgh, PA: Duquesne University Press, 1998.

-- *Time and the Other.* trans. Richard A. Cohen. Pittsburgh, PA: Duquesne University Press, 1987.
-- *Totality and Infinity.* trans. Alphonso Lingis. Pittsburgh, PA: Duquesne University Press, 1969.

Locke, John. *An Essay Concerning Human Understanding.* Amherst, NY: Prometheus Books, 1995.

Márquez, Gabriel García. *One Hundred Years of Solitude.* trans. Gregory Rabassa. New York: Harper Perennial Modern Classics, 2006.

Martin, Mike W. "Moral Creativity," *International Journal of Applied Philosophy* 20:1 (2006).

Martin, Raymond & John Barresi. "Introduction: Personal Identity and What Matters in Survival: An Historical Overview." *Personal Identity.* eds. Martin & Barresi. Malden, MA: Blackwell Publishing, 2003; 1—74.

Mbiti, John S. *African Religions and Philosophy*, 2nd ed. Oxford: Heinemann, 1989.

Mills, Charles. *Blackness Visible.* New York: Cornell University Press, 1998.

New English Bible with Apocrypha, The. New York: Cambridge University Press, 1972.

Nietzsche, Friedrich. *Basic Writings.* trans. Walter Kaufmann. New York: The Modern Library, 2000.

-- *The Portable Nietzsche.* trans. Walter Kaufmann. New York: Penguin Books, 1976.
-- *Untimely Meditations.* trans. R. J. Hollingdale, ed. Daniel Breazeale. New York: Cambridge University Press, 1997.

Nozick, Robert. *Philosophical Explanations*. Cambridge: Belknap Press, 1981.

Otto, Rudolf. "Buddhism and Christianity—Compared and Contrasted." Philip C. Almond trans. *Buddhist Christian Studies*, vol. 4 (1984); 87—101.

Parfit, Derek. *Reasons and Persons*. Oxford: Oxford University Press, 1986.

Plato. *The Complete Works*. ed. John M. Cooper & D. S. Hutchinson. Indianapolis, IN: Hackett Publishing, 1997.

Proust, Marcel. *In Search of Lost Time Vol. 1: Swann's Way*, trans. C. K. Scott Moncrieff & Terence Kilmartin. New York: The Modern Library, 2003.

Radhakrishna, S. "Introduction." *The Principle Upaniṣads*. New Delhi: HarperCollins India, 2007.

Ricoeur, Paul. *Conflict of Interpretation*. trans. Kathleen McLaughlin. Evanston, Il: Northwestern University Press, 1974.

-- *Fallible Man*. trans. Charles A. Kelbley. New York: Fordham University Press, 1985.

-- *Memory, History, Forgetting*. Trans. Kathleen Blamey & David Pellauer. Chicago: Chicago University Press, 2006.

-- *Oneself as Another*. trans. Kathleen Blamey. Chicago: University Chicago Press, 1994.

Russell, Bertrand. *Why I Am Not a Christian and other essays on religion and related subjects*. Ed. Paul Edwards. New York: Simon & Schuster, 1957.

Sartre, Jean-Paul. *Being and Nothingness*. trans. Hazel E. Barnes. New York: Washington Square Press, 1992.

-- *Search for a Method*. trans. Hazel E. Barnes. New York: Vintage Books, 1968.

Searle, John. *Mind: A Brief Introduction*, (New York: Oxford University Press, 2004).

Sophocles, *The Oedipus Tyrannus of Sophocles*. trans. Sir Richard Jebb. Cambridge: Cambridge University Press, 1887.

Strawson, Galen. "The Self." *Journal of Consciousness Studies* 4:5—6 (1997); 405—28.

-- "Postscript." *Personal Identity*. eds. Raymond Martin & John Barresi. Malden, MA: Blackwell Publishing, 2003.

Tengelyi, L. "Redescription and Refiguration of Reality in Ricoeur." *Research in Phenomenology* 37 (2007).

Tolstoy, Leo. *Confession*. trans. David Patterson. New York: W. W. Norton, 1996.

-- *War and Peace*. trans. Richard Peavar and Larissa Volokhonsky. New York: Alfred A Knopf, 2007.

Whitman, Walt. *Leaves of Grass*. New York: Bantam Classics, 1983.

Williams, Bernard. "The Self and the Future." *Philosophical Review* 79 (1970); 161—80.

Wright, Richard. *Black Boy*. New York: Harper Perennial Modern Classics, 2002.

ABOUT THE AUTHOR

Donovan Irven was born in Cumberland, Maryland, a small working class town in the Appalachians. He studied philosophy, history, and creative writing at Frostburg State University and received his Master's Degree in Philosophy from West Chester University of Pennsylvania. An American Philosophical Practitioner's Association Certified Philosophical Counselor, Donovan Irven resides in Philadelphia where he writes, practices philosophy, and is an Adjunct Instructor at several colleges and universities. You can follow him on Twitter @DonovanIrven, and contact him through Facebook, or his blog, *In the Time of Ethics* [http://inthetimeofethics.blogspot.com/]. *Two Days of Dying*, a novel, was Donovan Irven's first book. *The Ontological I & Other Essays* is his second book and his first public work in philosophy.

www.ingramcontent.com/pod-product-compliance
Lightning Source LLC
Chambersburg PA
CBHW022100090426
42743CB00008B/667